The Four Little Dragons

THE EDWIN O. REISCHAUER LECTURES, 1990

The Four Little Dragons

THE SPREAD OF INDUSTRIALIZATION IN EAST ASIA

Ezra F. Vogel

HARVARD UNIVERSITY PRESS

CAMBRIDGE, MASSACHUSETTS

LONDON, ENGLAND

Library of Congress Cataloging-in-Publication Data

Vogel, Ezra F.
    The four little dragons : the spread of industrialization in
East Asia / Ezra F. Vogel.
        p. cm.
    "The Edwin O. Reischauer lectures."—CIP half-t.p.
    Includes bibliographical references and index.
    ISBN 0–674–31525–1 (alk. paper) (cloth)
    ISBN 0–674–31526–X (pbk.)
    1. East Asia—Industries.   2. East Asia—Economic condi-
tions.
I. Title
HC460.5.V64   1991
338.095—dc20   74037   91–16051
                                                       CIP

To the memory of Tazuko Monane,
wonderful colleague and inspiring teacher
1939–1991

Contents

Preface

EDWIN REISCHAUER is well known for his work on Japan, but in fact he was dedicated to the study of all of East Asia. All of us who study this area of the world work from the foundation that he and John Fairbank laid. We feel toward these mentors what the Japanese call *on,* a sense of obligation—for their scholarship, for the institutions they built that make our task easier, and for the model they set as educators who communicate to a wide audience.

But thanks in no small part to the explosion of research they inspired, it is now harder to command all the relevant research on contemporary Asia, to say nothing of keeping up with the unprecedented changes in the real world we study. How can we provide perspective on a part of the world where, as Natsume Soseki's character Sanshiro observed of Tokyo eighty years ago, "everything looks as though it were being destroyed and rebuilt in the same moment"? I suspect that many of us studying East Asian industrialization know how Charlie Chaplin's comic figure felt when facing the industrial machinery in the film *Modern Times.* Like the subjects we study, we must constantly run to keep up with bewildering new technology and social changes that threaten to exceed our intellectual grasp. Though acutely aware of how much more I should know about so many topics, I will nevertheless try my best to emulate Ed Reischauer, to provide the kind of overview that he would have wanted to see.

FOR COMMENTS on an earlier draft, I thank Vincent Brandt, Carter Eckert, Thomas Gold, Huey-fen Lu, Gregory Noble, Byung-Nak Song, Edwin Winckler, and Yangsoo Yoo. For intellectual discussion of these issues, I am particularly indebted to a decade of talented teaching fellows in my core curriculum course on industrial East Asia. For editorial assistance I am grateful to Elizabeth Gretz and for bibliographic assistance to Nancy Hearst.

The Four Little Dragons

I A New Wave of Industrialization

IN EAST ASIA, the dragon has been a compelling symbol of power for over a millennium. Traditionally Asia's dragon throne was in China, but in the first part of the twentieth century Japan, by developing a superior industrial base, replaced China as Asia's leading power. In the first decade after its defeat in World War II Japan resumed its industrialization, progressing at a pace the world had never seen. Over the next three decades four nearby little dragons—Taiwan, South Korea, Hong Kong, and Singapore—modernized even more quickly. How did Japan and the four little dragons achieve such a rapid industrial transformation? Why did a few peninsulas and islands, dots on the East Asian periphery, gain such Promethean energy and accomplish so much at this particular time?

These five societies represent less than 1 percent of the world's land mass and less than 4 percent of the world's population. Yet together they have become, with Europe and North America, one of the three great pillars of the modern industrial world. As of 1988, Japan and the four little dragons constitute five of the world's seventeen top trading nations.[1] They have dominated the world's textile and electronics industries since the 1960s. Japan and South Korea have become the two largest shipbuilders in the world as well as formidable producers of steel and automobiles. Tokyo and Hong Kong have joined New York and London as the great financial centers of the world. The two economies with the largest foreign currency holdings in the world are Japan and Taiwan. Citizens and companies of Japan, Taiwan, South Korea, Hong Kong, and Singapore control a significant portion of the assets of Europe and North America, far more than Europeans or North Americans control in East Asia. And these five East Asian economies continue to grow faster than those elsewhere.

Yet until the 1930s, it was possible to view industrialization as a solely Western phenomenon. Even in the 1950s, leading scholars could argue that success in industrialization was related to a special ethos found in Protestantism or to other qualities unique to Western civilization. Some sought to analyze why, in East Asia, tradition "prevented" modernization. Even in the 1960s and later, when East Asian countries were already making their industrial breakthroughs, other scholars explained that the Western powers made less developed non-Western nations dependent on them, thus keeping them from industrializing.[2]

Since World War II, manufacturing plants have been built all over the globe, but aside from the West, only in East Asia has industrialization become so widespread that an entire nation's average standard of living and infrastructure have been raised to Western levels. In the 1990s, of the roughly five billion people in the world, almost one billion reside in industrialized societies. Of this one billion, 750 million live in the industrialized West and 200 million live in industrialized East Asia.

Now that industrial breakthroughs in East Asia have become so unmistakable, conflicting explanations have blossomed. Some scholars argue that East Asia proves the success of national industrial policy or of the strong developmental state, because in this era, despite the growth of world trade and multinational corporations, the nation remained the unit that guided and sustained industrial development. Others believe that the breakthroughs show only the success of free markets. Ardent East Asian nationalists point to the uniqueness of their tradition, while development planners point to universal features that provide lessons for others to follow.[3] My own approach to finding explanations will be inductive and in the end somewhat eclectic; I find no single theory or perspective adequate to explain the phenomena we observe.

Early, Late, and Late Late Industrialization

Of all the many aspects of modernization, I choose to concentrate on industrialization, the replacement of human labor by machinery to produce goods, not only because it sharpens the focus for comparative study, but because new industrial technology has been central to the transformation of the last four decades. It was, of course, new technology that enabled a worker to produce far more output with a given amount of labor; and it was industrial production, both for domestic use and for export, that generated the wealth necessary to raise the standard of living. Industrialization became a major goal of government activity, and factories moved the center of gravity of social life from the countryside to the towns and cities. But the significance of industrialization goes even further. As Karl Polanyi argued in *The Great Transformation*, the introduction of machinery was crucial both for creating a modern market economy and for giving rise to a basic belief in the efficacy of material commodities to resolve human problems, two changes that can be said to have altered the course of civilization.[4] Even the phrase "industrial society" indicates how fundamentally our thinking about ourselves and our society has been affected by the process of industrialization.

We use a single term, "industrial revolution," to describe

this process of change, but the industrial revolution initiated by England in the eighteenth century was far different from that undertaken by the four little dragons in the first four decades after World War II. Not only is manufacturing now far more advanced and complicated, but the organization of industry, from the extraction and transportation of raw materials to the production, distribution, and marketing of finished products, is now far more complex, requiring higher levels of technology and management skills.

Scholars such as Alexander Gershenkron, David Landes, and Ronald Dore have used the term "late developer" to describe the countries of continental Europe that in the late nineteenth century tried to catch up with the original industrializer, England. In England, and to some extent in the United States, industrial change had been more incremental. Workers there acquired additional skills on the job without special training programs. The capital requirements for these incremental improvements were modest by later standards, and much of the capital could be generated from within. Countries in continental Europe that initially fell far behind England and that later quickly tried to catch up skipped some of the steps that the pioneer had gone through, and sought to build from scratch new large-scale modern plants. These plans led to a sudden spurt of development and required large inputs of capital. To bridge the gap as speedily as possible, late developers resorted to formal training programs and centralized research institutes. The effort to build an infrastructure, acquire capital, train workers, and manage the relatively sudden social transition without severe social and political disruption demanded a high level of coordination that only governments could supply. The governments in these late developing countries, therefore, played a much larger role in their industrial revolutions than had been the case in England and North America.

By the 1950s, when the four little dragons began their quest to catch up, the gap between the industrialized world and less-developed countries had grown even larger. We might, therefore, refer to the little dragons as "late late developers." Japan, which until the 1930s lagged slightly behind the major continental European industrializers, may be regarded as the pioneer late late developer. The advance of technology forced late late developers to incorporate even more complex industrial systems and subspecialties than the late developers had introduced a few decades earlier; and this activity, in turn, required still higher levels of coordination. Late late developers needed even larger inputs from savings[5] and from borrowed capital for investment, and this in turn required a larger effort to acquire and absorb technology and producers' goods and more networks to establish worldwide market outlets. The Japanese, who excelled in managing this catch-up process, fashioned a government that could coordinate and facilitate industrialization and, when necessary, take a more activist role. Yet they managed to avoid the rigid planning controls that in socialist and other would-be late developers blocked the development of a strong private sector. On the contrary, East Asian governments spurred the development of firms that often had greater strength and staying power than those in Western "free market" economies.

Changing Technology and Its Impact

Although my focus is the social institutions that accompany industrialization, it is useful to consider how these are shaped by technology.[6] Beginning with the first industrial revolution, one might distinguish five major waves of new technology. The first wave, which spurred England's original industrialization, came from textiles, where successive improvements in machinery enabled manufacturing to replace handicrafts. The second wave, which occurred as continental Europe began trying to catch up, was the manufacture of iron and steel, which in turn drove the expansion of coal mining. New heavy industry required the transport of massive amounts of commodities, and this was made possible by the newly invented steam engine, incorporated in steamboats and railway engines. The third wave was driven by the discovery of internal combustion, making possible automobiles and trucks, the expansion of the oil and petrochemical industries, and the improvement of roads and highways. This wave began after the continental European countries had already taken some steps toward industrialization. The fourth wave, consumer electronics, came just as the four little dragons were starting to industrialize. The fifth wave began with computers and telecommunications just as the little dragons began to take off, and incorporated other advanced technology in biotechnology, optoelectronics, and new materials.

England began textile manufacturing using wool, but it was cotton that enabled the original industrial revolution to take off, because cotton fibers were strong enough to survive machine production and inexpensive cotton acreage could be increased more rapidly than could flocks of sheep. The four little dragons began their industrial revolution using cotton, but as their economies started to take off, durable synthetic fibers became available at low cost, and their supply could be expanded even more rapidly than could cotton crops. By then, the technology of textile production had stabilized, and textile machinery was available at modest cost. East Asian countries beginning their industrial breakthrough could afford such equipment and operate it profitably, taking advantage of their lower labor costs. This advantage was especially clear in the apparel industry, which is even more labor intensive than textile production.

The manufacture of steel and the steam engine, which triggered the development of heavy industry and enabled Germany and the United States to surpass England, required great amounts of capital. In East Asia, Hong Kong and Singapore considered themselves too small to undertake such a heavy investment. Even for South Korea, which boldly invested in heavy industry in the 1970s, it was a great strain. The internal combustion engine was by then well developed, however; and the railway, so central to the growth of industry in Europe and North America, had been succeeded by motor transport and highways at the time Taiwan and South Korea were beginning their breakthroughs. And because oil had already begun to replace coal in heavy industry by the 1950s, Taiwan and South Korea required less coal for heavy industry than earlier developers.

It was the new revolution in consumer electronics and household appliances that created special opportunities for East Asian industrialization. Electricity was in use throughout the world, and new inventions made possible a host of new consumer products. The rise in the standard of living in Western nations after World War II promoted the growth of mass markets. As with textiles, the investment required for modern machinery to produce electronic products was not great and large labor inputs were still needed, which favored countries with cheaper labor costs.

The new computer and telecommunications technology was important in a different way. Initially, East Asian countries did not produce this equipment on a large scale. Inventions in this sector, nevertheless, occurring just as these countries began to industrialize, hastened the flow of information around the world and thus enabled East Asia to gain quick access to technology and new markets.

After World War II, a newly industrializing country had access to all five waves of technology almost simultaneously. The steam engine, coal, and the railroad had been superseded, but newer versions of technology from the other waves were still useful. New industrializers could begin by acquiring relatively inexpensive machinery to manufacture textiles and household consumer items. They could then gradually make use of the new equipment for modern computers and telecommunications to increase their own efficiency. As capital accumulated and their organizational capacities attracted capital from home and abroad, they could purchase the production equipment needed for heavy industry.

New Opportunities after World War II

After World War II, the gap between industrialized and nonindustrialized nations had grown so large that a formidable effort was required to bridge it. Yet at the same time, a late late developer could acquire industrial skills and experience in world markets because of circumstances that had been nonexistent earlier.

The Cold War and Technology Sharing   It was above all the Cold War that led the preeminent industrial power, the United States, to allow and even encourage technology to flow to its allies. American leaders, preoccupied with stopping totalitarian expansion at its roots, were willing to offer economic and technical assistance to allies against communism. The United States was then so far ahead of any other major country in industrial technology and standard of living that it saw little threat in sharing its technology, investing its capital, and opening its markets to foreign products. Unlike an earlier era, when England had blocked the export of its industrial technology, the American military was prepared to share its advanced equipment with its allies, the American government did not block the private transfer of technology within the free world, and American universities welcomed foreign students.

The Expansion of International Trade   International trade and investment greatly expanded after the war, and the world trading system became far more open than it had ever been before. From the sixteenth century, when mercantilism began, until just after World War II, tariffs and customs had heavily restrained the international exchange of goods. Resources were not always available on the world market, and as an industrial nation developed its colonies, it kept control over colonial resources as well. International trade and investment had grown in the decades before World War I and had begun expanding again after World War I, but this growth had ended with the Smoot-Hawley Act of 1930, which intensified the world depression.

Just as the tragic global war that resulted from concessions to Hitler in Munich in 1938 made post-war planners determined to oppose any totalitarian aggression, so the disastrous depression, triggered at least in part by tariffs raised through the Smoot-Hawley Act, made planners determined to maintain an open world trading system. The United States took the lead in establishing the Bretton Woods Monetary Agreement of 1944, the General Agreement on Tariffs and Trade in 1947, and the Kennedy Round of Trade Negotiations from 1962 to 1967, all of which paved the way for an unprecedented expansion of world trade. The amount of trade was, of course, enhanced by great advances in transport and communication, by the readiness of investors to lend capital around the world, and by the absence of wars that interfered with trade. The value of American merchandise imports, for example, increased twentyfold between 1960 and 1985, from $15 billion to almost $340 billion. In 1960, the United States bought goods from Japan valued at a total of $1.1 billion; in 1985 the value had risen to $68.8 billion, an increase over sixty times in twenty-five years. U.S. imports as a percentage of total U.S. gross national product rose from less than 6 percent in 1960 to 22 percent in 1980.[7] In Europe and East Asia, other nations also greatly increased their participation in international trade. Smaller economies, in particular, benefited from the opportunity to enrich themselves by producing goods for world markets.

Growth of Mass Consumption   The rising standard of living in Europe and, especially, in North America greatly increased the purchasing power of ordinary families. With the growth of mass media and the mass society, more families wanted what David Riesman called the "standard package" of consumer items. In the United States, the expansion of the automobile and the highway made possible a revolution in marketing. As large department stores and mass marketing outlets replaced small neighborhood retail stores, it became easier to bring goods from great distances and sell them at low prices. New opportunities existed for countries that could produce goods in massive quantities for these outlets, an advantage especially important for small nations that lacked large domestic markets.

The Information Revolution   The growth of mass media and educational institutions and the creation of new international agencies greatly enhanced the ability of one nation to learn from another. The sheer increase in the publication of newspapers, magazines, newsletters, technical publications, and books sped up the transfer of knowledge. Perhaps just as important, the invention and rapid diffusion of television made quickly accessible to the people of the world a more nuanced understanding of the attitudes, practices, and information that underlay the technical aspects of industrialization. Never before had it been possible for such a high percentage of people outside the West to gain such an accurate understanding of so many aspects of the advanced countries of the world so quickly.

Opportunities for higher education also increased at a phenomenal rate after World War II. The rapid growth of the

American graduate school and its openness to foreign students made the secrets of industrialization more accessible to aspiring countries than in previous eras. To break into world markets in a period when industry had become so advanced required not only a mastery of science, engineering, and business management but an understanding of broader social and political developments. These topics became subjects of academic concern and were readily available to students around the world. The transfer of skills to guide industrialization was also enhanced by systematic programs begun by new institutions such as the World Bank and the International Monetary Fund.

The Emergence of Multinationals   As Western corporations expanded in size and established offices and plants in new locations, their commitment to their original community and nation atrophied. Western firms lessened their attachment to the work force in any particular locality. American-based multinational firms rationalized their activity, defining their purpose more precisely in terms of quarterly profits, thus loosening the social bonds with the community of which they had been a part. Large corporations were willing to produce, buy, sell, and lend anywhere in the world as long as their activity increased profit margins.

Americans, convinced of their nation's overall industrial and technological superiority, saw no need for a national economic policy promoting their interests over those of citizens elsewhere. Some interest groups pushed for the protection of a particular sector and achieved a measure of success. But they were balanced by a powerful consumer lobby that wanted the cheapest possible products, no matter who made them, by influential economists who believed in keeping markets open and reducing government interference, and by businessmen who profited from trade and investment. There was thus little pressure for a national policy to counterbalance firms that passed on technology, capital, and production to other parts of the world.

THE OPPORTUNITIES that the developed world, but above all the United States, provided as a source of technology and capital and as a market for products were open to any country in the so-called free world. Yet all the economies that achieved an industrial breakthrough in the first four decades after World War II were located in East Asia. How did Japan, Taiwan, South Korea, Hong Kong, and Singapore take advantage of these opportunities? How did each of them achieve the political unity and the will to push for industrialization? How did their governments facilitate the process and how did their firms develop the ability to produce competitive manufactured goods? The Japanese experience has been much studied, and therefore I will concentrate here on the four little dragons. The next three chapters focus on the particular features of industrialization in Taiwan, South Korea, and the two city states; in the final chapter I consider the common features of all the East Asian industrializers, including Japan.

2 *Taiwan*

TAIWAN WAS the first little dragon to achieve an industrial breakthrough. But in 1949, when Chiang Kai-shek retreated to Taiwan along with over one million mainlanders, the economic prospects did not seem bright. The island's bombing damage from World War II had been largely repaired and its GNP was approaching pre-war levels, but its average per capita income was still below $100 (U.S.) a year,[1] about the same as that of India. Except for some small textile factories, a few modern sugar refineries and other food-processing plants, Taiwan had no industrial base. After the Japanese surrender, moreover, Chinese authorities had transferred some of the little industrial equipment Taiwan did have to the mainland. As before the war, 60 percent of the island's work force was in agriculture. Inflation, which had destroyed public morale on the mainland, was not yet under control, and the sudden spurt in Taiwan's population from six to almost eight million between 1945 and 1949 made supply shortages more acute. Chiang and other top leaders had failed in their efforts to modernize the mainland, and just as their primary concerns before 1949 had been military, so after 1949 they were initially more preoccupied with retaking the mainland than with building up Taiwan. The world had not yet witnessed sustained rapid economic growth comparable to what was about to begin in East Asia, and no one in Taiwan could imagine the industrial transformation that was to occur in the decades ahead.

The Turn to a Self-Sufficient Economy

In 1949, to adapt to the changed international environment, the island's economy required fundamental restructuring. As a Japanese colony from 1895 to 1945, Taiwan had traded almost exclusively with Japan and Japan's other colonies, Korea and Manchuria. Taiwan had imported textiles and other industrial goods from Japan and had exported, in return, sugar, rice, and pineapples. After its defeat, Japan could no longer afford to buy Taiwan's exports, and even after Japan began its economic recovery, it lacked foreign exchange and chose to limit imports from Taiwan. Japan could get by with less of Taiwan's agricultural products because it had begun to receive American aid in the form of farm products through Public Law 480. In any case, Taiwan, with a population almost a third larger than in 1945, faced difficulty generating the agricultural surpluses that it had previously exported.

From 1945 to 1949, by reorienting its trade to mainland China, Taiwan was able to export some simple industrial products, but with Communist victory on the mainland, this trade was also cut off. Taiwan's goods were not then of sufficient quality to export to the West. Nor could Taiwan afford to satisfy pent-up local demand by importing foreign products.

The Kuomintang (Nationalist Party) leaders who arrived in Taiwan in 1949 dealt with this situation by trying to increase production to meet local demand. They sought to upgrade agriculture and to reorient the goods the island produced so that they would meet local needs. In short, the Kuomintang leaders pursued an "import substitution policy," the production locally of goods formerly imported, to make Taiwan a more self-sufficient economy.

Just as Taiwan began to concentrate on manufacturing basic consumer goods, however, its local industry was threatened by the massive outflow of cheap manufactured goods from Japan. In June 1949, therefore, Kuomintang leaders, to protect Taiwan's infant industries from the flood of low-priced Japanese products, established import restrictions.[2]

Of the consumer goods in short supply in Taiwan after the reduction of Japanese imports, textiles were most critical. Economic planners, therefore, concentrated on textile production, where local skills had been enriched by the arrival of several textile entrepreneurs from Shanghai and Shandong. Government strategists sought to maximize the value-added work done in Taiwan. As K. Y. Yin (Yin Chung-jung), the government's leading planner, put it, Taiwan's long-term advantage lay in importing "yarn rather than fabrics" and "cotton rather than yarn."[3] The government established import priorities that favored plant, equipment, and raw materials and supplied raw cotton to knitting mills in order to build up local industry that would meet local consumer demand. By 1952 Taiwan was producing its own cotton yarn and fabrics, and leaders turned their attention to producing bicycles, flour, cement, and other goods for which local demand was strong.[4]

The Kuomintang pursued their import substitution policy for a decade with great success. How could the Kuomintang, which failed so miserably in industrializing the mainland, have achieved such success in Taiwan?

Building Blocks for Industrialization

In Taiwan, the Kuomintang had several advantages, some fortuitous, some achieved by policy and effort, that helped make industrialization successful, both in the 1950s and later.

Political Stability Regardless of how misguided its earlier economic policies may have been,[5] in mainland China the Kuomintang failed fundamentally because it lacked the unity and stability necessary to attract capital for industrial development. In Taiwan, stability was easier to achieve, not only because the island was smaller and more manageable, but because Chiang Kai-shek brought to Taiwan a more unified leadership. To rule mainland China, he had been dependent on distant allies over whom he had little leverage. He had to cajole, pressure, balance factions, and sometimes fight to keep even a semblance of control.

When Chiang retreated to Taiwan, more distant regional warlords who had been his allies, such as General Li Tsung-jen, originally of Guangxi, did not join him. Troops not close to Chiang, such as those that fought on Hainan Island, were not permitted to come to Taiwan, and troops that did come to Taiwan were reorganized and more tightly unified by Chiang's most trusted military aide, General Ch'en Ch'eng. "Bureaucrat-capitalists" whom Chiang had difficulty controlling on the mainland, such as T. V. Soong and H. H. Kong, did not come to Taiwan. The highest officials who did join him were, for the most part, his personal followers from Zhejiang and other areas of the lower Yangtze and the top core of military leaders who had served under him when he was commander at the Whampoa Military Academy.[6] Chiang had firm authority because of his preeminence on the mainland and his control over the party, the army, and the government. In Taiwan, he quickly dissolved the party and military intelligence factions that contained potential rivals to his leadership, resisted American efforts to support officers trained in the United States, and effectively cultivated personal networks to maintain his control.[7]

After Ch'en Ch'eng died in 1965, Chiang Kai-shek's son Chiang Ching-kuo was his father's unrivaled heir. He had been uniquely trained for leadership by assignments in the economy, youth work, secret police, the military, and the party, and had already built up his own personal following.[8] After 1975, when his father died, until his own death in 1988, he dominated the Kuomintang Party, the military, and the government. Under both father and son some factional maneuvering and opposition existed, but never to a degree strong enough to interfere with the basic stability of the government.

The sense of threat from the mainland helped to sustain a high level of unity among Kuomintang leaders and to justify their tight control over the population. Party dominance was buttressed by the army and the secret police. After the Japanese colonial leaders had ruthlessly eliminated all serious resistance in the early years after 1895, the local population had become submissive. When the Japanese surrendered in 1945, some Taiwanese sought greater local autonomy, but this dream was brutally ended on February 28, 1947. On that day General Ch'en Yi, who had been dispatched to Taiwan as governor, responded to protests by slaughtering thousands of local residents, including many local Taiwanese leaders and university students.[9]

The replacement of Ch'en Yi and his public execution in Taipei did not eliminate the hostility between the newly arrived "mainlanders" and local Taiwanese. But the Kuomintang maintained a monopoly over the use of violence; and the local Taiwanese, who had not been reared to believe that a government existed to serve the will of the people, remained basically subservient, as they had been under the Japanese. Mainlanders dominated top positions in the government, party, and military until the late 1980s, although local Taiwanese were given considerable leeway in the development of local politics, and there was considerable progress in promoting local people to higher positions beginning in the late 1970s.[10] By that time Taiwan had begun to move, in Edwin Winckler's words, from a "hard authoritarianism," which relied explicitly on the army and the secret police, to a "soft authoritarianism," where force receded more to the background.[11] The Kuomintang did not initially win the hearts and minds of many local Taiwanese, but conversely, it was not under any obligation to local interest groups. Humanitarians at home and abroad criticized the way Taiwan achieved its unity, but it remains true that Taiwan's unity, though achieved by objectionable methods, gave modernizing bureaucrats more room to maneuver in promoting industrialization and gave capitalists confidence in the security of their investments in Taiwan's industry.

Control of Inflation and the Blossoming of Family Agriculture In their analysis of why they lost the mainland, Kuomintang leaders acknowledged that public support had eroded because of their failure to stop corruption and to provide for the common people's livelihood. Above all, they concluded, they should have done more to control inflation and implement land reform. They were determined to do better on Taiwan. They resolved to be strict with corruption, to expand the role of government enterprise in a way not susceptible to private influence, and to create a greater distance between the government and the private sector. Economic policymakers in Taiwan, for example, were not allowed to engage in their own businesses.

Inflationary pressures were reduced by a stable government, by the supply of goods through U.S. aid that began arriving in early 1951, and by the success of the policy to produce agricultural and manufactured goods to meet local demand. But these efforts were also aided by specific policies to control the money supply and to absorb liquidity by increasing interest rates for bank deposits.[12]

In mainland China after World War II the United States had helped establish the JCRR (Joint Sino-American Commission on Rural Reconstruction) to promote rural development, but

land reform had been difficult to implement because of the
objections of landlords, who were the backbone of the Kuomintang's rural support base. In Taiwan, because the Kuomintang was not beholden to local landlords, land reform
encountered no real political resistance. Land reform was considered so important for providing economic opportunities for
tenant farmers and for putting agriculture on a solid base that
Chiang's leading aide, Ch'en Ch'eng, personally took charge.
He began in 1949 with a rent reduction policy, followed by
the division of public land and the purchase of land owned by
large landlords, and then division to the tillers, all completed
by 1953.[13]

Unlike many developing countries, the government put great
stress on improving agriculture. As soon as land reform was
completed, officials worked through the JCRR, which they
had brought with them to Taiwan, to supply the newly independent peasants with fertilizers, pesticides, improved seeds,
technical advice, and credit. In providing such assistance, the
government was building on a solid base established by the
Japanese.[14] Because agriculture was so important, officials
in the JCRR were permitted a status and salary scale above
that of the regular bureaucracy, and half of American aid between 1951 and 1953 went for agriculture. The JCRR therefore recruited able young people[15] such as Lee Teng-hui, who
in 1988 became the first native-born president of Taiwan.[16]

Although planners in 1950 were not yet considering substantial industrialization, in retrospect it can be argued that
their concentration on agriculture helped prepare the way. An
ample supply of agricultural products helped keep down inflation, and valuable foreign currency did not have to be spent
for food imports. Production increased rapidly enough that
some refined sugar and other food products could even be
exported to earn additional foreign currency. In 1952 of
Taiwan's very modest exports, 22 percent were agricultural

products and 70 percent processed agricultural products; until 1959, nearly 90 percent of Taiwan's exports still consisted of agricultural goods and processed agricultural goods. Even in 1974, after industry had begun to take off, 16 percent of Taiwan's exports were derived from agriculture. As agricultural production increased, farmers could buy more manufactured goods and provide the state with a source of savings that could be used for industrial investment.[17]

Moderately Well Developed Infrastructure and Human Resources Unlike many colonial powers, Japan, during its occupation of Taiwan (1895–1945) and Korea (1910–1945), had made vigorous efforts to transform the colonies into modern countries. As Mark Peattie and others have demonstrated, Japanese leaders such as Goto Shimpei, who guided Japan's colonial policy in Taiwan after 1895, had shared the same ethos as the state-building modernizers at home.[18] To be sure, Taiwan's progress lagged far behind Japan's, and it was the 300,000 Japanese who were in Taiwan by 1945, some 5 percent of the population, who occupied the top positions in business as well as government. Chinese patriots may be correct in arguing that Taiwan might have developed even more rapidly without Japanese occupation, for China had begun to modernize Taiwan in 1884. But the fact is that Japanese colonialists introduced what were at the time modern railways, a modern telephone and communications grid, a modern banking system, a highly developed commercial market network, an effective public health system, and an extensive rural irrigation system.[19]

Perhaps even more important under the Japanese occupation were the development of local organizations, such as village cooperatives, and the expansion of literacy and technical training. From 1915 to 1944 the population of Taiwan increased from four to six million, but the number of children enrolled in Taiwan common schools increased from 66,000 to 798,000;

and by 1944, nearly three-fourths of Taiwan's children of elementary school age were in school.[20] By 1949 nearly half the population was literate.

Taiwanese under Japanese rule were exposed to railroads and telephones, to modern banking, and to a legal system that protected individual rights and private property. Some Taiwanese worked in large modern sugar factories built by the Japanese. Others worked for Japanese who were exporting rice, bananas, and sugar to Japan, and even the farmers who produced these crops gained experience in a commercial economy.[21] Local Taiwanese who served under the Japanese at least gained familiarity with such organizations. And during World War II, as Japan became preoccupied with its war efforts and imports of manufactured consumer goods from Japan began to fall off, local Taiwanese gained more experience in industry. The war forced Japan to allow some import substitution. And as Japanese men were taken from Taiwan offices to fight in the armed forces, the Taiwanese had an opportunity to rise somewhat higher in the bureaucratic and commercial hierarchies.[22]

The U.S. aid program from 1951 to 1965 also played a major role in providing industrial goods, plant, and equipment and other material aid which amounted to as much as 10 percent of Taiwan's gross national product in 1951, gradually declining to 2 percent in 1965 as the gross national product itself greatly expanded. Even more important was the U.S. role in training political leaders and government technocrats to help guide economic development and in encouraging them to give development a higher priority. By 1962 the World Bank, impressed with Taiwan's creditworthiness, began developmental assistance on a commercial basis.[23]

The combination of a population already well trained under Japanese colonial rule and mainlander technocrats eager to absorb new information with the rapid expansion of literacy and technical training provided a critical base for industrial development. As S. C. Hsieh and Lee Teng-hui later said, "the main secret of Taiwan's development was not her ability to meet the technological requirements for increasingly productive gadgets, but her ability to meet the organizational requirements of new combinations . . . of mutually helpful behavior necessary to achieve the gadgets."[24] Japanese colonialism and American aid had played a critical role in increasing this capacity.

The Will to Industrialize for Export, 1958–1960

By the mid-1950s the building blocks were in place and industry had made a good start in producing for local consumption, but this progress did not automatically lead to a decision to put more resources into industrialization in order to promote exports. In Taiwan, as in Japan and the other little dragons, there were debates at early stages of industrial development between industrial planners who wanted to move ahead quickly and financial specialists who, fearing inflation and the burden of debt, urged caution in industrial and infrastructure investments. In Taiwan, because of the disastrous experience with inflation on the mainland, cautious financial planners continued to have great influence, setting interest rates high and restricting investment. But by 1958 those who pushed for more industrial investment and export promotion policies began to win the day. Why?

By then local markets were already saturated with goods produced for import substitution, and after the mid-1950s the economy had become increasingly stagnant. Many goods could not yet be produced locally, the demand for foreign imports remained higher than the supply of locally produced exports, and it had become clear that growth in agricultural exports was reaching a plateau. Internationally, mainland

China's failure to invade Taiwan during the 1958 Taiwan Straits crisis and the opening rift in Sino-Soviet relations had reduced the sense of threat to Taiwan. The United States wanted to hasten the end of its economic aid to Taiwan, but it also wanted to leave Taiwan strong, a model of economic development for the Third World. And Chiang Kai-shek, concerned about the ending of American aid and aware that the immediate military threat had receded, was ready to concentrate on building a strong economic base that would enable Taiwan to buy or produce weapons to defend itself in the long run. To buy technology and new production machinery, Taiwan needed foreign exchange that could only be obtained by expanding industrial exports.[25]

In late 1959, American officials made it clear to Taiwan they were prepared to support the drive for industrial growth and a focus on exports if Taiwan would mobilize all available domestic resources, concentrate on domestic development more than on preparations to retake the mainland, and reduce government controls on the free operation of markets. Taiwan agreed and, early in 1960, announced a Nineteen Point Program for Economic and Financial Reform that included an expanded four-year economic plan for 1961–1964 and a program of incentives for private businesses that produced and marketed for export.[26] The effort to expand the economic base for an independent Taiwan proved successful, and in 1965 the United States ceased funding any new aid programs.

Among officials in Taiwan, there was a continuing tension between those who, like their leader Chiang Kai-shek, were preoccupied with retaking the mainland and those primarily concerned with local economic development. Because the goal of retaking the mainland remained an article of faith, Taiwanese economic bureaucrats until the 1980s could not publicize long-term visions that did not include an eventual return to the mainland. But in 1953 industrial planners were allowed to spell out for Taiwan Province a four-year "plan" that listed high priority projects in which government leadership was critical. In 1961 the third four-year plan, which incorporated the new efforts to produce for exports and introduced more elaborate planning with macroeconomic analysis,[27] paid little more than lip service to the goal of retaking the mainland. Local industrial development had become the focus of attention and pride.

The Super-Technocrats' Perspective

Officially, the Kuomintang Central Standing Committee made final decisions on economic policy, but in fact in the decades that followed 1949 a group of technically trained officials was given unusual authority to guide industrial development. How did these super-technocrats come to acquire this power and how did they approach their task?

Although Chiang Kai-shek had been trained as a military leader, he and other military and Kuomintang officials realized that economic matters required skilled specialists. In 1949, to coordinate the manufacturing efforts of diverse ministries, a central Taiwan Production Board was established, with Ch'en Ch'eng as chairman and K. Y. Yin, a trained engineer who had served from 1941 to 1946 as the director of the Chinese Foreign Trade Office in New York, as vice chairman and de facto director. Yin not only worked well with Chiang Kai-shek and Ch'en Ch'eng, but because of his experience in New York, it was natural that he become the principal liaison with the United States as its aid became a crucial factor. Although American leaders defined their national interest in Taiwan primarily in terms of security concerns, the key American activity on Taiwan was administered by AID (the Agency for International Development) and directed by specialists on economic development. Technocrats from Taiwan, the United

States, the World Bank, and the International Monetary Fund worked closely together.

Because of strong American reaction to the corruption in the distribution of American aid to China from 1945 to 1949 through UNRRA (the United Nations Relief and Rehabilitation Administration), Congress made it clear to Taiwan that continued U.S. aid was dependent on tight control over corruption. This strengthened the leverage of Taiwan technocrats against political interference.[28] The combination of a super-ministerial unit to coordinate other ministries, centralized control over U.S. aid, American support for independent technocrats, and Chiang's confidence in Yin enabled him to play a unique role as a super-technocrat guiding industrialization.

By the early 1950s, K. T. Li (Li Kuo-ting), trained in physics, had emerged as Yin's key assistant, and from 1963, when Yin died, until the late 1980s, Li was the preeminent super-technocrat. Yin and Li held many different posts, sometimes several concurrently. Yin was vice chairman under Ch'en Ch'eng in the Agency for Economic Planning and in 1950 also became the president of the Central Trust of China; when the Production Board was absorbed in the Economic Stabilization Board, Yin convened its Industrial Development Council. Li served under Yin on the Industrial Development Council and then as secretary general of the Council for U.S. Aid from 1958 to 1963, as economics minister from 1965 to 1969, as finance minister from 1969 to 1976, and as minister of state without portfolio from 1976 until 1989. Because of their ability, experience, dedication, and force of personality and because they enjoyed the confidence of Chiang Kai-shek, Yin and Li dominated industrial planning regardless of the positions they held. From Chiang Ching-kuo's perspective Li was not easy to manage, for he was the same age as Chiang Ching-kuo, the two men had first entered the cabinet at the same time, and Li was exceedingly forthright in expressing his views.

Chiang Ching-kuo did not treat Li as a member of his political inner circle. He did acknowledge Li's professional skills, however, and eventually adjusted to his preeminence on economic issues.

Yin and Li were highly pragmatic. They were fluent in English, well acquainted with foreign scientific and technical developments, and attuned to issues involving the broader social, political, and historical context. Their decisions about whether to support projects were made less by financial balance sheets and more by their estimate of Taiwan's technological and managerial capacities and their sense of overall historical trends. They had a sense of responsibility for the fate of Taiwan, and they cultivated talented people under them who held most of the important positions in the economy for four decades.[29]

The economic bureaucrats recruited by Yin and Li and by their counterparts who guided financial policies were among the ablest, best-educated people in Taiwan. Of Taiwan's top forty-four economic planners in the 1950s and 1960s, forty-three were university graduates; 52 percent had advanced degrees from the United States and 9 percent advanced degrees from Europe.[30]

Many of these senior bureaucrats had excellent training and experience even before they came to Taiwan. In the late 1930s some of China's most talented planners, including Yin and Li, had served on the National Resources Commission, where they began to apply scientific management to expand and modernize state industrial enterprises. During World War II hundreds of promising scientists and engineers in China were sent to the United States and Europe for advanced training in preparation for major administrative roles in post-war China. As William Kirby has found in tracing their careers, the main beneficiary of the training program after 1949 was Taiwan. Those who remained on the mainland played only a minor role in economic policy, but the substantial group who in 1949 left China for Taiwan played major roles and proved to be very effective.[31]

For guidance on technical issues of macroeconomic policy, the government drew not only on local economists but on a talented group of Chinese-born economists who held major academic posts in the United States, including Sho-chieh Tsiang and Ta-chung Liu of Cornell, John Fei of Yale, and Gregory Chow of Princeton. These economists visited Taiwan frequently and worked closely with leading economists there such as Wang Tso-jung.[32] Through their advocacy of reducing tariffs and import restrictions, reducing foreign exchange controls, and revaluing currency to market levels, they helped play a role in hastening Taiwan's relaxation of governmental controls and adaptation to international markets.

However, those who played the major role in shaping Taiwan's industrial development and national economic strategy had, like Li and Yin, been originally trained not as economists but as engineers and scientists. From 1949 to 1985, ten of the fourteen ministers of economic affairs had been trained in engineering.[33]

One could argue that the engineers and scientists turned bureaucrats who surrounded Yin and Li and dominated economic policymaking played a role much like that of good traditional Confucian advisors, but both their style and the content of their work were new in Chinese history.[34] They were part of the world scientific and development communities, and they believed in growth and progress. Unlike the economists, who stressed market forces, they believed in the importance of social engineering, and particularly in the important role of government in helping to acquire technology, allocate funds for key projects, and guide the development of the economy. In the party and the military, influence was affected by personal connections, but among these bureaucratic planners and among the economists as well, influence depended less on personal connections than on others' estimates of their capabilities and respect for their commitment to the public good. Some were at times suspected of using their public position for private gain and some at times elevated personal rivalries to political squabbles, but in general the bureaucrats were regarded by foreign observers as dedicated professionals who did not leak public goods into private hands or distort public policy to achieve private aims.

Government bureaucrats were familiar with Japan's basic export strategy. Yin had taken a special interest in the Meiji Restoration and spent three months in Japan on a study tour in 1950. Like their Japanese counterparts, Taiwan's bureaucrats realized that they had few natural resources and that their population had grown rapidly. They believed that like Japan, Taiwan must expand its manufactured exports to survive. They realized that they needed to improve both their productivity and the quality of their output. Japan's successes in breaking into foreign markets helped stimulate Taiwanese bureaucrats to emulate the basic Japanese approach to export promotion. They protected infant industries from foreign competition and worked to limit the extent of foreign control of businesses in Taiwan. They tried to restrict borrowing from abroad to critical technology and infrastructure projects. And, as they observed that in Japan higher wages eventually reduced competitiveness in certain sectors, they hastened to help Taiwanese firms in those sectors replace Japanese firms in world markets.

Because all of Taiwan's high officials had come from the mainland, however, they were not fluent in Japanese or familiar with the details of the Japanese approach. Local Taiwanese businesses were able to apply their Japanese-language skills and experience with Japanese merchants during the colonial period to their interactions with the Japanese businessmen who began returning to Taiwan in the 1950s. But for leading officials, detailed thinking about how to guide the island's development came overwhelmingly from the United States.

The Government Approach to Industrialization

How did these talented former engineers and scientists go about promoting industrialization?[35] Initially, they saw their major responsibility as building up state enterprises. In 1949, few private entrepreneurs had the skills and resources to guide modern industry, and the technocrats, aware that state firms were on the rise in Europe, believed that they were the key to progress. All sizable industrial establishments in Taiwan before 1945 were Japanese owned and in 1945 all of them, whether private or public, had been taken over by the Chinese government; by 1946, they were reorganized and consolidated into twenty-two state firms.

Government officials who managed these firms often had good technical training but did not always have the first-hand managerial skills and the entrepreneurial imagination to make them efficient and profitable. Within the government some officials, encouraged by American advisors, argued that some of these firms could do better under private management, and in 1953, private entrepreneurs who had acquired more skills and capital were allowed to buy certain firms. During the 1950s, however, even while some firms were being privatized, in other key sectors, such as steel, shipbuilding, electric power, and nuclear power, new state firms were established. Still, over time there was rapid growth in the private sector. In 1949 the private sector accounted for only 28 percent of production value, but by 1985 it had grown to 84 percent.[36] With the exception of certain critical sectors, the government gave up managing firms directly and specialized in guiding development.

In the early years after 1949, the government played a very direct role even in managing the private sector. With tight import restrictions, almost no firms had the foreign exchange to buy imported commodities, which were largely supplied by U.S. aid. The Taiwan government took these commodities and in effect placed them on consignment with the private firms that could make best use of them, thus reducing the financial burden and financial risk to firms then woefully short of capital.

From this base, the government moved to provide basic commodities for private enterprises. Early on it adopted a strategy of producing basic goods such as cotton, iron, steel, and refined petroleum in state firms, and then selling these products cheaply to private firms as a way of driving industries such as textiles, machinery, fertilizer, and plastics that by the 1960s could produce for export. China Petroleum, for example, provided chemical products for synthetic fibers to the textile industry, and beginning in the late 1970s, China Steel provided low-cost steel to the machinery industries. Like public companies elsewhere, few were profitable. Nevertheless, managers and engineers who had been well trained in the United States introduced modern management systems, and some, such as Chao Yao-tung of China Steel, trained at MIT, succeeded in creating profitable and efficient state companies.

As leaders became more convinced that the private sector could prove more vigorous in more areas, they helped develop private businesses. In 1957, for example, the government helped shape a new company to produce artificial fibers for the textile industry. In one of the most famous cases, the government sought a private firm willing to take over a government PVC (polyvinyl chloride) plant originally financed by AID to help develop the plastics industry. After some difficulty in locating a promising entrepreneur to take the job, the government in 1957 settled on a determined entrepreneur then dealing in lumber in Japan, Y. C. Wang, who began to build Formosa Plastics into the world's largest PVC maker and reputedly became Taiwan's richest businessman. He too helped supply artificial fiber to help drive the textile industry. To launch such crucial ventures the government ensured the sources of supply and the availability of credit.[37]

Chiang Kai-shek wanted to build up heavy industry and electronics that could support a defense effort, and these considerations as well as market demand affected decisions.[38] The government built a large integrated steel plant as soon as it was convinced that domestic demand was sufficient to absorb it, and it supported mini-steel mills when it considered them appropriate to meet market demands.[39] As Taiwan became independent of American aid, and especially after 1972 when the United States opened up relations with mainland China, Taiwan officials began to increase investment in the steel and chemical industries as a way to help the defense sector.[40] Taiwan wavered on whether to develop an automobile industry but, after some hesitation and changes of heart, decided that Taiwan had too small a domestic market to develop a profitable automobile plant. It opted instead to ally with foreign auto firms to produce certain auto parts on a scale sufficient to be competitive in world markets.

Of course, to develop key sectors and promote exports Taiwan also used tax incentives and proprietary loans and assisted in technology transfer. To eliminate red tape so that Taiwan could compete with Hong Kong in attracting overseas Chinese capital in producing goods for export, Taiwan opened the world's first export-processing zone in Kaohsiung in 1966. Later a second zone was opened near Kaohsiung and a third in Taichung. To promote high-tech development Taiwan developed the Hsinchu Science and Industry Park in the late 1970s.

From the beginning, bureaucrats wanted to improve the transportation and communications infrastructure, but those responsible for finance were cautious about taking on such expensive projects before they were confident that growth would generate revenues to repay the investment. Reinforcing river banks and dikes, building roads and bridges, and generating electricity were major tasks of the 1950s and 1960s. In 1973, after the economy was already growing rapidly and infrastructure bottlenecks had developed, the government launched the Ten Major Development Projects, which helped to modernize highways, railways, and ports as well as to create large government plants in steel, shipbuilding, petrochemicals, and nuclear power. The projects were completed in 1979, whereupon the government announced twelve new projects, and in 1985 it launched fourteen more. In all cases continued growth more than repaid the investments. Increasingly, however, the major government activities were directed toward facilitating the growth of private companies, providing the infrastructure, technology, low-cost capital, and export incentives that private enterprise could take advantage of.

In the mid-1960s, in response to growing foreign pressure, government officials allowed direct foreign investment to increase. In the 1970s, as Taiwan grew more concerned about its increasing loss of formal diplomatic relations and feared isolation, it sought more investments from multinational corporations to enhance its political security and stem capital flight by deepening foreign commitment to its future. As a result, direct foreign investment, earlier almost nonexistent, began to expand rapidly.

Government–Business Relations

How, in a society that stressed *guanxi,* networks of personal relationships, did bureaucrats manage to avoid becoming captives of local business interests? In part they succeeded because in the 1950s they had relatively little contact with local business. The bureaucracy was aided by the fact that those in business were, as Thomas Gold says, considered subordinate to economic bureaucrats and were therefore responsive to bureaucratic pressure.[41] Implicit was the fact that most government officials were mainlanders, and most businesspeople were locals. When they met officially, it was expected that the government would convey directives to the business associations more than vice versa.[42] Bureaucrats received adequate compensation for their work, and beyond that most of them considered professional pride and public reputation to outweigh concern for personal material gain.

The Kuomintang could play a role not possible in the political parties of the West. Not only were promising young people in business and the bureaucracy members of the Kuomintang, but some were selected for special training programs. The effort can be seen negatively, as political cooptation, or positively, as linking the business community to the broader moral community concerned with overall public goals. Those in business selected for these training programs could later be assumed to be civic-minded and responsive to government guidance.

But the preservation of the public interest against personal relations still required some vigilance. By the early 1950s the managerial revolution had already taken place in Japan, and large Japanese companies and the Japanese bureaucracy worked with each other more as representatives of organizations than as personal acquaintances. It could be assumed that when bureaucrats met with company officials, the latter were not seeking personal gain. This was not yet taken for granted in Taiwan, where firms were overwhelmingly run by first-generation founders. Chiang Ching-kuo, aware of the corruption that existed on the mainland, insisted that government bureaucrats not only refrain from accepting presents and dinner invitations from those in business but avoid any social functions at which members of the business community were present. Although these detailed regulations were considered annoyingly strict by many participants, they did curtail corruption and helped maintain a level of public support and trust before government–business relationships could be institutionalized on a nonpersonal basis.

Entrepreneurs

Where did the entrepreneurial skills come from that permitted such rapid growth in the private sector? The largest textile manufacturers who fled China in 1949 settled in Hong Kong, but a number of smaller ones, from the Shanghai area and Shandong, fled to Taiwan, where they initially produced goods on consignment from the government. Many used their initial successes in textiles to branch out in other fields. In 1976, for example, 33 of the top 106 business groups still had a textile firm at their core.[43]

But most "mainlanders," especially government and army officers, considered government service a superior calling, and they left private entrepreneurial opportunities to the local Taiwanese. Only later, when local companies became large, modern corporations with opportunities for white-collar managers, did mainlanders and their children consider the private sector respectable. In his study of 512 businessmen listed in Taiwan's 1982 *Who's Who*, Alan Liu found that 302 were Taiwan born and 210 were "mainlanders." The mainlanders tended to be concentrated in banking and textiles; the Taiwan-born were more often in food processing, electronics, plastics, and machinery.[44]

Some local Taiwanese businessmen had already gotten a start under the Japanese. As Thomas Gold has pointed out, when the Kuomintang instituted land reform, some of the more enterprising former landlords used the payment they received for their land to invest in private companies.[45] Independent farm families learned commercial skills by marketing their produce, and as they saved money, some opened their own businesses. Others began as employees of private enterprise, acquired skills, and after they had accumulated sufficient savings and their children were old enough to help in a family business, opened their own enterprises.[46] Although individual families relied heavily on their own savings to start or expand enterprises, many also borrowed from friends and relatives or, in the rural areas, from local credit associations.[47] The number of small businesses increased rapidly in the 1960s and 1970s. Between 1961 and 1971, for example, the number of enterprises employing between 10 and 500 employees tripled, and the number of workers more than tripled from 184,000 to 654,000, a rate of increase even greater than in firms employing more than 500 people. These small and medium-sized enterprises continue to play a major role in Taiwan's overall manufacturing capacity, far more than in South Korea, where the government encouraged the concentration of business assets in a small number of very large firms. From the perspective of small-business owners, the Taiwanese government, despite its efforts and its contribution to infrastructure, technology transfer, and export market promotion, has not been instrumental in their success. Not unlike businesspeople elsewhere, they believe they did it on their own.

To meet large foreign orders for goods, a number of small factories often formed linkages so that together they could produce goods in sufficient quantities. This mechanism also reduced the risks for an individual company, which need not be completely dependent on supplying a single large customer. As industries began producing more complex products, many assemblers relied heavily on subcontractors for various parts, which gave them similar flexibility to expand or contract without requiring large capital investment and without risking enormous losses at a time of downturn.

Edwin Winckler suggests that the most important agents of Taiwan's export-oriented industrialization may have been the American buyer and the representative from the large Japanese trading firm. With the expansion of mass marketing and discount stores in the United States that began in the 1950s, American buyers and officials of Japanese trading firms scoured the world for low-priced goods. A buyer could sit in a Taipei hotel bar, and a local businessman would bring in his samples. If the businessman seemed promising but lacked technology, the buyer could arrange to send out engineers from America to share technology, inspect the products, and ensure timely delivery. U.S. manufacturers who assembled goods also scoured the world looking for inexpensive parts, and they offered Taiwan businesses similar opportunities.

The intriguing question is: Why were Taiwanese businesses on the average more willing and better able to fill the orders of American buyers than the businesses of Latin America, Africa, and elsewhere? Although more systematic research is needed, it is clear that the people in resource-poor Taiwan were in general more eager than their counterparts in other parts of the world to respond to these opportunities. They had relatively high levels of education and, comparing themselves with citizens in Western countries, seemed more actively dissatisfied with their present circumstances than some counterparts elsewhere. They were prepared to work hard for wages that by Western standards were extremely low. Although the buyer may have had difficulty ensuring that the producers met all the specifications in a timely fashion, the producers quickly acquired at least some measure of responsibility in meeting deadlines and quality specifications. Taiwanese businesses could accept large orders beyond their own capacity, confident that other Taiwan companies or subcontractors would help them fill the orders on time. They were eager to acquire skills that would provide greater long-term opportunity and willing to accept modest life styles so earnings could be reinvested in new manufacturing equipment. And the supportive government network of information about technology and international markets helped make local entrepreneurs aware of new opportunities.

By the 1980s, a significant number of entrepreneurs were passing on the leadership of their companies to a second generation. Until that time family ownership had been the dominant form of enterprise, and the first generation tended to retain a paternalistic style of management even if the firm grew large.[48] Familism had strong roots in the Taiwanese farm family, but even the farm family often split upon succession,[49] and the same was true for business families. Paternalism is not unique to East Asia, but the willingness to learn and sacrifice in order to accumulate wealth for future generations is perhaps stronger in most East Asian societies than elsewhere.

Only in the 1980s, with the passing of some first-generation owners, did professional management blossom and ownership become separated from control in a substantial number of companies. Many of the second generation had received advanced training in the United States in such fields as engineering and business administration, and when they returned to Taiwan, they helped their family companies absorb higher levels of technology. The second generation did not necessarily return to Taiwan immediately upon completing their overseas studies; often they remained in the West to work for some years. Until the 1970s even Taiwan bureaucrats whose children were studying abroad bemoaned this loss of talent, failing to foresee the role that these students would later play in Taiwan's development. In the 1980s, as the level of technology in Taiwan rose, the island was able to absorb many with higher levels of training. By the time the Hsinchu Science Park was established in the late 1970s, many of the advanced scientists who had remained in the United States at universities, in corporate research labs, or even in design and engineering work were returning to Taiwan or helping their families or friends there to establish new companies. Some who remained in their American companies managed to assign subcontracts to former classmates working in Taiwanese companies. Taiwanese leaders no longer viewed these emigrés as a "brain drain" but as an investment in a "brain bank," which could be drawn on as Taiwanese companies became better able to absorb more advanced technology.

The multinationals that set up manufacturing operations in Taiwan beginning in the mid-1960s, after the resolution of the Taiwan Straits crisis reduced political risk, were mostly seeking cheaper labor to produce goods they had previously made elsewhere until labor costs rose too high. As Thomas Gold has noted, Taiwan's government and entrepreneurs successfully avoided being overwhelmed by multinationals.[50] The determination of the Taiwan government to protect infant industries, to introduce new technologies, and to limit foreign investment while generating its own internal savings rate helped provide the leeway for local firms to gain strength without being displaced by foreign multinationals. Indeed, in addition to the several hundred thousand vital small companies, Formosa Plastics became the world's largest PVC maker, Evergreen the world's largest shipping container company, and Acer a world-class company in high technology.

The Transformation of Society and Politics

The industrial transformation that had taken Western nations and Japan a century, or even longer, was completed in Taiwan in essentially four decades. In this time, the annual per capita income rose from less than $100 (U.S.) to over $7500. By the end of the four decades, Taiwan's infrastructure was in the range of that of modern Western societies. The government's success and cautious financial policies enabled Taiwan to pass Germany to become second only to Japan in the possession of foreign currency. Taiwan retained a solid base of industrial production, but with more efficient production equipment, the percentage of workers engaged in industry peaked at 42 percent and began to decline by the early 1980s.[51] The society had been largely rural in 1949, but at the end of the next four decades nearly half the population was living in the metropolitan areas of Taipei, Kaohsiung, and Taichung,[52] and most of the rural population had been linked to nearby urban areas and transformed by urban culture.

Some problems remained in the infrastructure, which was not yet completely transformed, and serious new problems had been created by the sudden rush to industrialization. The island had too long neglected severe problems of traffic congestion and environmental pollution, which only in the late 1980s began to receive the attention they deserved.[53]

In the fourth decade, just as its industrial breakthrough was nearing completion, Taiwan's international situation fundamentally changed, owing to its loss of international recognition and the growing thaw in the Cold War. During the 1970s Taiwan lost many of its seats in international bodies to mainland China, and in 1979 the United States recognized mainland China and de-recognized Taiwan. No other government with such a sizable economy had so little formal international representation. The loss of formal diplomatic status created new anxieties and accelerated the effort to strengthen economic and cultural ties around the world.

As tensions between the Kuomintang and the Communists diminished, Taiwan in 1987 allowed its citizens to visit mainland China and permitted some trade between the mainland and Taiwan. Although in the early 1990s trade was still officially indirect, Taiwan's trade and investment in the mainland were growing rapidly. Within the first two years after the opening of travel to the mainland, an estimated 600,000 from Taiwan had visited. But the substantial rise in the standard of living in Taiwan through industrialization had created far larger social and economic gaps between the people living in Taiwan and those living in the mainland than had existed in 1949. The Kuomintang lost the military battle with the mainland in 1949, but in effect won the economic battle in the following decades. The thaw and the size of the economic gap has raised questions in Taiwan about the pace and nature of growing economic ties with the mainland and the shape that a resolution of political issues might take.

Unlike the Communist world, Taiwan loosened its tight political control and responded to calls for democratization after its industrial breakthrough rather than before. In Taiwan, the economic advances and the relatively equal distribution of wealth in the first decades of industrial growth had created a measure of popular support for the government that was absent in many countries where the popular strivings for a higher standard of living had not yet been met. Taiwan's equal distribution of wealth benefited from land reform, from high levels of universal public education, from the widespread opportunities for employment in the nation's many labor-intensive industries, and from the dispersal of small businesses to all parts of the country.[54]

At the end of four decades, Taiwan's political system had not yet been fully transformed or stabilized. The strong governmental institutions that had been built and adapted to guide the process of industrialization were clearly still in place, despite the great advances in democratization. These highly centralized governmental institutions enabled the state to exercise strong leadership in many spheres. In the area of pollution, for example, Taiwan, which had one of the most serious situations in the world in the late 1980s, had the prospect of being a world leader in pollution control before the end of the 1990s.

The authoritarian leaders and experienced super-technocrats who guided industrial development were by the late 1980s giving way to increasingly democratic politicians and specialized technocrats. The industrial transformation the original leaders had helped launch, however, had left a legacy of a highly educated population and a widely distributed pattern of wealth as well as strong governmental leadership, a legacy that was likely to continue beyond the transformation of Taiwan into an industrialized society.

3 *South Korea*

LIKE TAIWAN, South Korea on the eve of industrialization was part of a divided country preoccupied with a Communist military threat.[1] It, too, had experienced Japanese colonialism, through which it had gained some infrastructure, a higher level of literacy, and experience with modern commerce. After its civil war, South Korea worked closely with the United States, which provided guidance and assistance. South Korea had few natural resources, and with an expanding population, twice the size of Taiwan's, it too needed to export to survive. Its population, like Taiwan's, was largely rural, ready to move to urban areas and to work for wages lower than those paid for similar work in Western countries.

The Devastation of the Korean War

But the problems South Korea faced were far more serious than Taiwan's. South Korea had been devastated by the Korean War. The Chinese Civil War had been fought on the mainland, sparing Taiwan, but the Korean War, arguably the most destructive war in world history, devastated South Korea as well as North Korea. Seoul changed hands four times, each time with bitter fighting. Only a small portion of the country, in the southeast, had not been invaded by the North. Of the twenty million people in South Korea when the war ended in 1953, about a fourth were refugees with no home, almost no assets, and, unlike Chinese mainlanders who came to Taiwan, little hope of finding secure employment. Over one million civilians and 320,000 soldiers in the South lost their lives. A disproportionate number of the dead were able-bodied young men who, had they lived, would have contributed to the work force and to their families' incomes.

In 1953 South Korea had even less of an industrial base than Taiwan had had in 1949. South Korea did not reach a GNP of $100 per year until 1963,[2] a decade later than Taiwan. In Taiwan, the Japanese had built up some of the world's largest, most modern sugar refineries and other food-processing factories. In Korea, the Japanese had tamed the Yalu River in the 1930s by building enormous hydroelectric stations, which generated 90 percent of all of Korea's electricity, and nearby they erected large chemical factories for the production of fertilizer and munitions. But when the country was divided, all of these facilities went to North Korea. South Korea, until then the nation's bread-basket, had little electric power and little industry aside from textiles.

Although Taiwan and South Korea were each parts of divided countries, Taiwan had long been a distinct administrative unit, and since 1889 an independent province. As an island it had a natural economic coherence and a clear political jurisdiction, with well-established relationships between counties and the provincial capital. In Korea, the new boundary at the 38th parallel split the country artificially into two halves that under Japanese rule had developed a complementary economy. The new boundaries divided families, friendships, and administrative structures as well as the economy. Political leaders who had begun in the late 1940s to develop national linkages now had to build a base only in the South. Firms had to reorient their supply lines and markets.

Building Blocks for Industrialization

Like Taiwan, South Korea began to industrialize with several important building blocks already in place. Some of them were achieved through great hardship, but all in one way or another contributed to the country's ability to modernize.

Forced Unity Japan's colonial leaders had given neither Koreans nor Taiwanese a chance to rise to positions of real leadership, and Korea had no one who compared with Taiwan's mainland refugee leaders, fully experienced in thinking about national issues. Syngman Rhee, who dominated South Korean politics from the end of World War II until 1960, was a proven patriot. He had been imprisoned from 1898 to 1904 for nationalist activity, and had long defended Korean causes in international bodies such as the League of Nations. Having received an M.A. from Harvard in 1908 and a Ph.D. under Woodrow Wilson at Princeton in 1910, he, like his contemporary Yoshida Shigeru in Japan, was a determined anti-Communist who knew how to handle American superiors. But when he returned to Korea with an Austrian wife in 1945 after an absence of almost forty years, he had few social roots in his native land.[3] In the turmoil of a nation suddenly free from the tight control of Japanese colonialists but without a clear direction and badly split between pro- and anti-Communist groups, he had the determination and manipulative skills needed to retain power. But, lacking an independent power base, he succeeded by resorting to intrigue, intimidation, patronage, and reliance on experienced policemen who were disliked because they had collaborated with the Japanese; he enjoyed little popular support.[4] Unlike Chiang Kai-shek, Rhee brought with him no well-organized staff experienced in governance, and neither he nor those under him had a vision for industrial modernization.

Since the latter part of the nineteenth century, Korea had been disrupted by political protests and upheavals to a far greater degree than had Taiwan. Protest movements often advance social justice and humane government, but they do not appeal to investors considering building or expanding factories. Compared with the Taiwanese, who responded to colonialism with subservience, Korean hostility remained nearer the surface. Koreans resisted more vigorously than the Taiwanese, and when the Japanese responded with tougher military repression, Korean nationalism grew still more determined. In the spring of 1919, the Japanese cracked down on the Korean independence movement, killing an estimated 7,500 and wounding some 16,000. Koreans made the incident a powerful symbol of the hated oppressor. The Korean Christian Church, which the Japanese could not suppress completely for fear of angering the international community, served as a locus of simmering opposition to tight government control during, but also after, Japanese occupation.[5] In 1945 the South Korean reaction to former Japanese collaborators was more severe than in Taiwan, and even in 1990 the passion for retribution had not fully dissipated.

Taiwan was little troubled by Communist opponents on Taiwan itself, because they had remained on the mainland; but in South Korea, before the Korean War, many villages had been split between Communist sympathizers and their opponents,[6] and with the relocation of several million refugees after the war, unrest continued. In the late 1950s public disturbances against Syngman Rhee swelled until they toppled his government in April 1960.[7] The massive demonstrations that brought down Syngman Rhee left a profound impact on national consciousness, both among those who struggled against successive military governments and among the rulers who worried that mass movements might lead to their own demise.

Many Chinese and Westerners criticized the leadership of Chiang Kai-shek, but after he retreated to Taiwan no one really challenged his rule or, later, that of his son, Chiang Ching-kuo. South Korea had no such preeminent leader to stand above rivals and thus achieve an easy unity. Park Chung Hee seized power in 1961 via a military coup and reinforced his control by active repression of the potentially explosive opposition. To many people frightened that disunity would leave the South vulnerable to attack by the North, however, the use of force seemed necessary, though not fully legitimate.[8]

Fear of the North not only made the South's forced unity more palatable but helped intensify the drive for industrialization. The aggressiveness of the North seemed unbounded and its behavior unpredictable. After the country was divided, the North began with a bigger industrial base, had the benefit of Soviet aid, had no difficulty restraining private consumption, and put over 15 percent of its gross national product into the military. South Korea's capital city was only thirty miles from the border, and North Korean propaganda was unrelenting. Over the years newly dug tunnels under the demilitarized zone were discovered. Occasional incidents, including the 1983 attempt in Burma to assassinate the South's president with a bomb that did kill several South Korean cabinet members, sharpened the public's fear. The determination of the United States in the 1960s to wind down economic assistance, followed in the 1970s by the Nixon Doctrine, which reduced America's military presence in Asia, and by Carter's announced desire to remove U.S. troops from Korea, provided a powerful stimulus for Korea to seek an independent industrial base adequate to support its own national defense efforts.[9]

Disciplined and Motivated Human Resources　In its efforts to industrialize, South Korea did possess, in addition to its greater size, several distinct advantages over Taiwan. Among these were a highly disciplined population, a sharper national consciousness, and a stronger national vitality.

Even after the Korean War, all able-bodied men served over two years in the military. The South Korean military leadership was very different from that in Latin America, the Philippines, and other nations that had not fought a modern war. As in many other developing countries where jobs were scarce, the permanent army attracted many talented youth, many of whom had become impatient for faster promotion and faster national progress by the late 1950s.[10] In addition, since the Korean War was an all-out modern war, the Korean military was not only familiar with the latest military technology but had learned, as Vincent Brandt has pointed out, to handle modern machinery and to manage complex logistical support systems using modern transport and communications.[11] Even after the war ended, the American military, fearing a renewed attack from the North, continued to provide the South with modern technology and modern logistical training.[12] Because the bitterness of the Korean War had helped forge a clear sense of purpose and because virtually all men had been subject to military training, the South Korean male population was highly disciplined during their country's period of rapid economic growth.

Korean determination and vitality may not be precisely measurable, but they are nonetheless real. The nation's determination clearly hardened as a result of repressive Japanese colonialism and the fierce Korean War, but it also grew firmer as South Koreans gained confidence from their economic success. At the peak of Japan's rapid growth rate, the average Japanese never worked as much as 50 hours a week. During South Korea's rapid growth, the work week approached 60 hours a week, and in the late 1980s it continued to average about 55 hours, 10 hours more per week than in any other industrial or industrializing country. South Korea began its industrialization push in 1965 with far lower technology and far lower wages than Japan had in 1955,[13] and thus achieved industrial competitiveness with greater individual effort. In Middle East construction projects, Korean workers were without rivals in their willingness to work long hours in a scorching climate. Among the American allies fighting in the Vietnam War, the Koreans were known as the most determined fighters. In recent years many Japanese lament the decline of the American work ethic, but their comments about Koreans resemble American complaints about Japanese: "The Koreans" some Japanese say, "work incredibly long hours, from morning to night, like robots. They have a 'hungry spirit' and are constantly stealing our industrial secrets."

Koreans approach education with the same fervor. At the time of independence from Japan nearly half of all Koreans were illiterate, but no country has made more rapid strides in education,[14] especially in higher education. And no nation's youth has been more fervent in pursuing knowledge and information, primarily in the United States and Japan but also in Europe and elsewhere. South Korean students are second to none in preparation for their university entrance examinations. The number of Korean students in graduate school in the United States and Japan combined has been greater than from any other country, and a high proportion have returned to their homeland, especially in recent years when their skills have been in great demand. Koreans have gathered information not only in science and engineering but also in economics and other social sciences, and in the humanities. They thus have acquired not only specific information, but a broader sense of historical development.[15]

Knowledge of Japan   No country approaches South Korea in detailed knowledge of Japanese government, business, technology, and even language. Local Taiwanese learned Japanese during the occupation, but the top leaders in Taiwan, who came from the mainland, had not; in Korea in 1953, by contrast, all well-educated adults knew Japanese. Under Japanese rule Koreans had not occupied top positions in the government or in large corporations, but some had learned about large organizations in holding lower positions and others had led small companies that did business with Japanese firms.[16] In 1990, 250,000 South Korean high school students were studying the Japanese language, constituting approximately 70 percent of all the non-Japanese high school students around the world studying Japanese.[17] Park Chung Hee, who ruled South Korea from 1961 to 1979, attended a Japanese military academy and served two years as a lieutenant in the Manchurian Army in World War II.[18] He and many of his generation not only had a good sense of Japanese organization, but maintained close personal relationships in Japan. After economic growth began in the mid-1960s, in addition to the closeness of Pusan, Korea, to Shimonoseki, Japan, and the availability of Japanese radio, television, and printed media, close contact with many of the 600,000 to 700,000 Koreans who remained in Japan gave Koreans unrivaled access to Japanese information.

Because of both the depth of Japanese penetration and the repressive nature of Japanese colonialism, Korea has an even deeper ambivalence toward its former colonial masters than do many other one-time colonies. Japanese public opinion polls for decades reported its citizens' most disliked nations to be the Soviet Union and Korea, and if anything, Korea more than reciprocated this hostility. Koreans condemned the brutality and exploitation of the Japanese during their occupation, the massacre of Koreans in Japan after the earthquake in 1923, and the slave-like treatment of Korean miners forcibly taken to Japan. They were enraged at the continued reluctance of Japan to grant citizenship to second- and third-generation

Koreans living in Japan, or to apologize for past wrongdoings, or to treat Koreans with basic respect. Yet many Koreans, even in colonial times, had been accepted into Japanese elite circles and institutions, including universities, banks, and government offices, and took pride in their mastery of the Japanese language and culture. An intense ambivalence has resulted, leading Koreans to bitter denunciations of Japan and making it difficult for many to acknowledge the underlying admiration that they feel toward Japan. The ambivalence of Koreans is perhaps best described as not "love and hate" but "respect and hate." In any case, in sector after sector, no nation has profited more from an understanding of Japanese success than South Korea.[19]

Efficient Agriculture　After liberation from Japanese rule, the South Koreans, like the Taiwanese, carried out land reform and undertook, with American support, a lively program to improve agriculture. In 1961, when industrialization began, roughly two-fifths of Korea's gross national product derived from agriculture,[20] and agriculture still centered around rice cultivation.[21] In the years after the Korean War, agricultural production increased much more rapidly than it had before World War II.[22] By the 1970s South Korea had achieved the highest rice yields per hectare of any country in the world. As in Taiwan, agricultural productivity not only made food imports unnecessary, but allowed some farmers to start industrial workshops.[23]

The Government Approach to Industrialization

The Korean push toward industrialization began in earnest in 1961, almost a decade after Taiwan's industrialization began. South Korea's effort to industrialize brought together a strong military ruler dedicated to economic development, some entrepreneurial young military officers,[24] a talented but inexperienced bureaucracy, a broad base of disciplined citizens who were ready to work to build an economic base to defend against the North, and a national determination to match Japanese successes.

When Park Chung Hee seized power in May 1961, he was determined that after the end of American aid South Korea become able to produce the goods required for national defense.[25] He wanted to improve the life of the common people suffering from poverty, and he realized that he needed economic progress to defend his political base against those who regarded his seizure of power as illegitimate. He made economic progress a mission.[26] In his first hundred days, he moved to establish an Economic Planning Board to coordinate rapid development and announced that the first five-year plan would begin in January 1962.[27]

Eager for industrial development and aware that, as America began pulling out, South Korea would have to export in order to buy the equipment to produce its own goods, Park in 1961 immediately began to promote industrial production for export. Taiwan, which had turned to an export-oriented policy only two years before, had for a decade been pursuing an import substitution policy, but South Korea, in its haste, immediately launched export-oriented industrial development when import substitution was still in its early stages. The government began issuing export targets to firms and supplying resources to help them realize the targets; and the firms worked to comply. In 1962 South Korea exported goods worth $42 million, less than one-fourth the value of Taiwan's exports at the time, and only $9 million of the Korean exports were in manufactured goods. By 1970 Korea exported $1 billion worth of goods, and by 1981 $20 billion, virtually all in manufactured goods.[28]

At the very top, Park selected a small group of able business executives and economic technocrats with whom he met regularly. He also began meeting with a group of about fifty academic advisors, but, finding some of their advice impractical, he soon dissolved this group and hired a few of them as aides on his Supreme Council. He acquired a reputation for accepting advice from knowledgeable people, learning quickly, and doing what needed to be done for the economy. The government was small enough that important decisions remained highly centralized. If Chiang Kai-shek resembled a chairman of the board who allowed his super-technocrats considerable autonomy in developing the economy, Park Chung Hee was more like a front-line commander who made important decisions himself.

Some of Park Chung Hee's earliest supporters were military commanders, originally from North Korea, who had served with him in the Manchurian Army. But he and many of those who became his closest co-workers, businessmen as well as military men, had come originally from Kyongsang-do, in the southeast corner of the Korean peninsula. Park grew up near Taegu, the first major stop north of the port at Pusan on the main rail route to Seoul built by the Japanese and later extended into Manchuria. By the time Park came to adulthood the area was quite commercialized, with a strong Japanese influence; he and his associates thus grew up with a better understanding of economic development than did Koreans from most other localities.[29] Park often went through friends to choose advisors he felt he could trust, but unlike Syngman Rhee, he was strong enough to resist less able friends who wanted rewards and selected people who could do the job.

The major foreign economic advisors to South Korea from the end of the Korean War until 1965 were Americans. Americans played a role in improving agriculture and in rebuilding the roads and bridges, shoring up riverbanks, increasing electric power, and importing new technology.[30] By the mid-1960s, as the United States brought its massive aid program to an end and as Park began to normalize South Korea's relationship with Japan, the role of Japan quickly increased in importance. Japan began to extend loans, and Park and his associates began to turn to Japan for technology, for manufacturing equipment, and for an overall model for development. However, concern over anti-Japanese sentiments that erupted in 1965, when students demonstrated against Park for resuming relations with Japan, prompted government officials to understate the actual closeness of South Korea's economic relations with Japan.[31]

Korean leaders had a cultural background similar to that of the Japanese, and with a country that was also a poor late late developer without resources, they adopted organizations strikingly similar to Japan's. The Korean Finance Ministry and Ministry of Trade and Industry looked very much like Japan's Ministry of Finance and MITI. To promote foreign trade, MITI had established JETRO (the Japan External Trade Organization), and South Korea established KOTRA (the Korea Overseas Trade Association). To manage technology introduced from abroad, MITI had established AIST (the Agency for Industrial Science and Technology), and South Korea established KIST (the Korean Institute for Science and Technology). Japan early on had a Reconstruction Bank that was later replaced by the Japan Development Bank. South Korea also initially had a Reconstruction Bank that was later renamed the Korean Development Bank. South Korea founded a Federation of Korean Industries similar to Japan's Federation of Economic Organizations (Keidanren) to deal with general management issues and a Korean Employers' Association similar to the Japan Federation of Employers' Association (Nikkeiren) to deal with labor issues. After Japan set up the Japan Economic Institute in Washington, D.C., to provide information to American officials, South Korea set up a Korean Economic Institute there with similar goals.

In some ways the institutions that the Koreans adopted resembled more the Japanese institutions that they had known through colonialism in the 1930s and 1940s than Japan's post-war variants. The Korean *chaebol,* about which more will be said below, were completely owned holding companies, like those of the Japanese *zaibatsu* before their dissolution in 1947. Unlike Japan's post-war Economic Planning Agency, which engaged only in indicative planning, Korea's Economic Planning Board exercised tighter control over planning, more like Japan's control associations during World War II.[32] Public banks in South Korea dominated finance, much like the banks Korea had experienced during Japan's colonial rule. The Korean CIA exercised very tight control over dissidents and political opposition, more reminiscent of pre-war than post-war Japan. The role of the politician in South Korea remained very limited until the late 1980s, much like that of the pre-war Japanese politician. South Korea had tight control over labor unions, much like Japan before the war, and labor disruption rarely occurred except when political authority was relaxed, as in 1959–1960, 1979–1980, and 1987.[33]

Unlike post-war Japanese industrial policy, which stemmed from large sectoral associations with structured relationships with corresponding government bureaus, sizable Korean companies were relatively few in the early stages of industrialization in the 1960s and 1970s. Government officials guiding the economy were also few, and therefore South Korean industrial policy was more tightly centralized, as in wartime Japan. As in Japan and Taiwan, the central government bureaucrats concerned with the economy were selected from a small pool of the nation's most talented and best-educated citizens, and these bureaucrats were considered by foreign specialists to be a highly dedicated group of professionals who did not use their positions in pursuit of personal gain.

In Japan, the government had established model textile

plants in the 1870s and a modern steel plant in 1900. Japan entered the modern chemical and electronics industries at the time of World War I. In the 1950s, although Japan was short of material goods because of the war, it still had engineers, managers, and workers who had technical and organizational experience that permitted the nation to move ahead in a deliberately planned way.

Korea began its industrialization with a far lower technical base and a far lower standard of living. Because there had been little industry aside from textiles in the southern half of the country before the Korean War, South Korea lacked experienced engineers and managers to help with the rebuilding. Determined to gallop ahead at the fastest possible speed, the Korean government borrowed heavily from abroad. Japan and Taiwan, by contrast, invested more slowly, relying more on domestic savings. South Koreans embarked on projects even before all the plans or the necessary technology were solidly in place and then extemporized, working to the limits of their endurance to solve whatever problems arose. Sometimes fast action was required, and in such situations South Korea benefited from its centralized hierarchical structure and an activist president who acted decisively and implemented plans without delay. South Korea was not as receptive to direct foreign investment as Taiwan, which, as it began to lose formal diplomatic status in the 1970s, felt it needed foreign investment to help secure its international status. And with economic affairs tightly controlled by ambitious officials on the Economic Planning Board, Korea's industrial investment was less constrained by cautious financial bureaucrats than in Taiwan—at least until the late 1970s, when Korea's macroeconomists began to assume greater responsibility for controlling inflation.

Despite these differences in approach, South Korea, like Taiwan and Japan, began modernization by strengthening agriculture and infrastructure and then moved to industrial production. In the early 1960s South Korea moved quickly to produce fertilizer in order to replace what had formerly come from the North or from abroad, and this in turn required building up electric power and oil refining. It also began to produce agricultural machinery and to strengthen the country's infrastructure by improving highways, ports, and communications. With urbanization, the nation began to develop an urban infrastructure;[34] and as industrial productivity moved ahead of agricultural productivity, it sought in the 1960s and 1970s to carry on rural community organization work to encourage rural development[35] without burdening the national budget. In the consumer goods sector, South Korea quickly tried to produce its own goods for daily use rather than relying on imports, and before 1961 it had already made great progress in reducing the proportion of imports that were consumer goods and increasing those that were used to expand industrial capacity.[36] It promoted the manufacture of textiles, apparel, athletic shoes, and later electronics for export. With a smaller economy than Japan's, it could not rely as much on its domestic market and became far more dependent on exports than Japan.[37] It tried to upgrade technology both to expand the scale of exports and to improve productivity, seeking to remain internationally competitive while raising wages.

Initially, because South Korea was unable to produce its own manufacturing equipment and process its own raw materials, it imported industrial supplies from Japan. In textiles, for example, chemical fiber or the feedstock for the fibers were initially imported. Eager to move ahead but lacking their own technology, South Korea's electronic and machinery industries often began as assembly plants for parts produced in Japan.[38] When Koreans began to build ships, not only the crankshafts but the entire engines came from Japan. But as quickly as possible Koreans learned to make more of the parts for the products they assembled, and then went on to assemble more complex products, again importing from Japan the parts they could not yet produce. With far fewer technicians and far fewer companies than in Japan, the Koreans could not produce as broad a range of products, and therefore concentrated in a small number of promising areas. As Koreans gained experience in producing a given product, they continued to narrow or eliminate the quality gap with Japan.

But South Korea's need to import parts and equipment from Japan created a large trade imbalance between the two countries. Japanese bureaucrats, anxious to hasten their nation's transition to higher technology, encouraged Japanese companies to cede products at the low end of the technology scale to countries such as South Korea. In practice, however, Japanese companies, observing the hollowing out of American industry, tried hard to continue producing as much as they could at home. Until the late 1980s Japan bought almost no manufactured goods from South Korea. South Korea's trade balance with Japan remained in the red; but because South Korea exported products to the United States, throughout most of the 1980s it came close to balancing its trade accounts.[39]

From the beginning of their industrialization drive, Koreans were preoccupied with the fear of Japanese domination of their economy and with the reluctance of Japanese companies to part with their technology. South Korea, like Japan in the 1960s when it was preoccupied with American domination, kept strict control over Japanese direct investment, Japanese capital, and Japanese products. South Korea also protected its infant industries until they were of very substantial size, and even then resisted opening its markets to foreign products. South Korea remained one of the few countries that imported virtually no Japanese cars, a policy that Japan reciprocated when South Korea began producing cars that were competitive in international markets. Through constant vigilance at all levels, Korean bureaucrats and business leaders were successful in keeping down the level of Japanese direct investment and preventing Japanese financial domination. The Korean experience contrasts sharply, of course, with the situation in the United States and Southeast Asia, where Japanese direct investment grew rapidly beginning in the late 1980s. Koreans eagerly sought Japanese technology, but they fought, as the Japanese had fought earlier, to keep control in their own hands.

Japanese companies, having observed the experience of American industry, have been far more cautious about sharing technology with other countries for fear it might lead to what they call the "boomerang," that is, the return of products using that technology into their own markets. Yet some Japanese have been willing to share their technology under certain circumstances, as when Koreans have other options of acquiring technology from their competitors, Japanese or foreign. Even when the Japanese have been reluctant to share, they have been unable to stop the flow of technology completely. Many Westerners gave up on acquiring technology from the Japanese, but the Koreans persisted, acquiring far more technology from the Japanese than from Americans and far more than most Westerners believed possible.

In some cases, Koreans simply licensed technology or purchased the right to use patents.[40] They were also assiduous in their study of publicly available information. In the 1980s, hundreds of Koreans gained admission each year to Japanese technological institutes and university engineering programs. For graduate education, Koreans more often went to the United States. At one point, for example, roughly half of the thirty graduate students majoring in shipbuilding at MIT were Koreans.

In the case of steel, a group of enlightened Japanese business leaders, headed by Shigeo Nagano, decided that having peaceful international relations in East Asia required economic health in other countries. Thus New Japan Steel helped by selling its technology to establish the great Korean steel plant at Pohang, which began producing steel in 1973. By 1983 Pohang was producing nine million metric tons of crude steel a year, far more than produced by Taiwan.[41] At Pohang, the layout of the plant, the management organization and style, the machinery, and even the uniforms worn by the steel engineers are virtually indistinguishable from those in large Japanese steel plants. In the late 1980s, as the South Korean steel industry improved more rapidly than the Japanese had expected, the successors of Shigeo Nagano were reluctant to share more of their technology. For their new rounds of steel modernization in the late 1980s and early 1990s, therefore, the Koreans turned to the Europeans.

When South Koreans purchased machinery from the Japanese, they bargained to learn as much as possible about parts and repair techniques. They worked as partners and suppliers to Japanese firms. They invited Japanese consultants, retirees, and others who for whatever reason were willing to share technology and paid them cash for the knowledge thus acquired. Like the Japanese, the Koreans engaged in "reverse engineering," carefully taking apart successful foreign products in order to study them and create products similar to the original. South Korea was unrivaled, even by Japan, in the speed with which it went from having almost no industrial technology to taking its place among the world's industrialized nations.

As soon as it was able to borrow the necessary capital in the late 1960s, South Korea decided to expand into heavy and chemical industries. It pursued the program throughout the 1970s, although the projects required large-scale indebtedness to foreign institutions and led to inflation.[42] South Korea's first heavy industry products entered the marketplace just after the first oil shock, when the world entered a recession. In the late 1970s, therefore, unable to sell enough of its production to repay its loans, South Korea experienced severe economic difficulties. At first, as Korea expanded its heavy industry in the early 1970s, some Taiwanese leaders feared they were falling far behind. Later, as South Korea's trade imbalances and debts ballooned, the Taiwanese were relieved that they had been more prudent and that they had moved so quickly to repay their international loans. But despite its problems, Korea's heavy industry program got back on track in the early 1980s. South Korea continued to pursue a heavy industry effort in steel, shipbuilding, and automobiles. Although they borrowed heavily to finance this expansion, a brief window of opportunity that lasted from 1985, when the Japanese yen rose substantially against the dollar, until 1988, when the Korean won rose against the dollar, enabled Koreans to make substantial progress in repaying their loans.

Entrepreneurs

Korea's Economic Planning Board and Ministry of Trade and Industry gave far more detailed directives to Korean companies than Taiwan's government gave to its companies. Through tight control of banking, the South Korean government could determine which companies received which loans at what rate. But it was the firms themselves that were responsible for profits and losses.

South Korean planners observed how Japan in the 1960s prepared for the inevitable opening of its markets as a result of foreign pressures. Japan moved to increase the size of its companies to enable them to produce competitive goods on a large scale and thus keep out imports through market forces. Koreans became convinced that to compete on international markets and withstand the threat of foreign imports, they, too, would need large companies. Unlike Taiwan, which was content, with some notable exceptions, to allow small firms to compete on their own, the Korean government actively pushed its successful firms to hasten their increase in scale.

In the aftermath of the Korean War, industry was largely centered in the southeastern cities of Taegu and Pusan, both because these had been developed by the Japanese and because these were the only major urban areas that had not fallen to the North. Park Chung Hee and his associates selected highly successful firms with proven entrepreneurs and provided them with low-interest government loans, tax incentives, and whatever other resources were necessary to strengthen them to become strong diversified *chaebol*, tightly controlled by a holding company. Since the *chaebol* firms were almost entirely new, founded in the post-war period, they differed from the mature Japanese *zaibatsu*. In Japan, Mitsubishi had been in business a century, Sumitomo and Mitsui several centuries. Even before World War II, when the *zaibatsu* were still controlled by holding companies, ownership had been separated from control. But in South Korea, even in the late 1980s, over forty of the top fifty *chaebol* were still firmly controlled by the original founder.[43]

The founder had generally gotten his start in a profitable business in a single sector such as rice milling, food processing, construction, commerce, textiles, or real estate. As business proved successful, the entrepreneur began to diversify into new and promising areas, often borrowing to expand to take advantage of growth opportunities. The founders were strong leaders; their circumstances required much initiative, bold vision, and forceful and quick responses. As with the great founders in many countries, success and experience strengthened their self-confidence and also their inclination to make all final or critical decisions by themselves. If anything, *chaebol* founders tended to be bolder than their counterparts in most countries because the government stood behind them, ready to help.

The initiative for companies to expand into new sectors sometimes came from the government, which tightly controlled the financial institutions. This situation differed from that of pre-war Japanese *zaibatsu*, each of which had its own bank. When state planners believed it possible to open up an important new sector, they encouraged companies with appropriate managerial and technical capabilities. In a new sector or major product line, they tried to encourage the development of at least two major companies so that competition between them would reduce the danger of monopoly and provide the same kind of focused competition between companies that existed in Japan.[44] When companies failed, government officials offered incentives to encourage others to take them over in order to avoid problems of unemployment. The large diversified *chaebol* thus expanded much more rapidly than they would have under market forces alone.

One sector that played a uniquely important role in the growth of *chaebol* was construction. After the Korean War, the reconstruction of roads, railroads, riverbanks, port facilities, and public buildings was an urgent priority. Americans supplied modern construction equipment, which Koreans quickly mastered. During the Vietnam War, when America sought contractors for construction work in Vietnam, Korean companies, by then experienced in working with the U.S. military, were often the lowest bidders. After the oil shock of 1973, oil-producing countries, rich in new-found wealth and lacking in skilled engineers and willing workers, contracted out projects to foreign construction companies. Korean *chaebol* performed well and won a large share of civil construction bids. In 1979 there were sixty-eight Korean companies and 93,000 Korean workers in Saudi Arabia alone. Two-thirds of the Korean construction workers were former soldiers, highly disciplined, familiar with modern machinery, and accustomed to barracks life. They willingly worked long hours to earn far more than they could in their impoverished home areas. Korean *chaebol* such as Hyundae, Daelim, and Dong Ah experienced explosive growth because of their success in Middle East construction, and some small companies grew large enough to become *chaebol*. For almost a decade these companies thus collectively generated billions of dollars of foreign exchange annually with which to expand their industrial bases at home.

Post-war Japanese *zaibatsu* executives were salaried employees who did not become terribly wealthy. Some family owners of Korean *chaebol,* by contrast, acquired considerable wealth, although many plowed substantial proceeds back into their businesses. Until the late 1980s, the gap between South Korean blue-collar and white-collar wage scales remained large in comparison with Japan's. In some *chaebol,* owners were criticized as being part of a regional clique from the Taegu (Kyongsang-do) area that also included prominent political figures. Inside information concerning how these *chaebol* acquired some of their funds has not been made fully public; and the businessmen involved have been vulnerable to charges of favoritism and the government to charges of corruption. At the same time, however, no one has doubted that the *chaebol* founders were very effective and hard-working entrepreneurs.

Like pre-war Japanese *zaibatsu,* the Korean *chaebol* generally consisted of a diverse group of companies in different sectors, controlled by a single holding company. The founder of a *chaebol* usually placed relatives in charge of the important affiliated companies and subsidiaries in order to maintain reliable personal control. Turnover of blue-collar workers was, throughout three decades of growth, high compared with that of Japanese companies. Loyalty was not yet highly developed and workers moved quickly when expanding companies, short of skilled managers and technicians, offered substantially better conditions to lure workers away. Other workers, as in Taiwan, saved from their modest salaries, and as they acquired skills, found ways to borrow from friends to establish their own businesses. Although white-collar turnover was also high by Japanese standards, by the 1980s the larger *chaebol* had begun to develop, as in Japan, a professional white-collar staff, with seniority, long-term employment prospects, and a better benefit package than that of small companies. Still, because of concern with loyalty, the owners often had a small core of especially trusted employees and family members who were on a faster track than ordinary white-collar employees.[45] Only in the late 1980s, with rapid expansion and the passing of the founder generation, did most *chaebol* begin to undergo a managerial revolution. Nonetheless, the second generation of the *chaebol* family often continued to occupy key positions that were not yet open to less trusted salaried managers.[46]

LIKE TAIWAN, South Korea also developed a highly successful, diversified, and dynamic small-business sector, which took advantage of new opportunities. As in Japan, when the economy began to produce more complex products, such as automobiles, that required more parts and suppliers, many small Korean manufacturers, to gain secure customers and upgrade their technology, began to affiliate with the large "parent" manufacturers. As in Japan and Taiwan, workers in these small firms, often relatives of the owner, were willing to work long hours at relatively low wages, giving flexibility to the large firms in adapting to business cycles and making a significant overall contribution to the vitality of the economy.

Yet of all the little dragons, South Korea has had the greatest concentration of large firms and the most ambitious goals, the

result of its fear of being overwhelmed militarily, by the unpredictable regime across the 38th parallel, and economically, by
the highly predictable Japanese economic powerhouse across
the straits. No nation has tried harder and come so far so
quickly, from handicrafts to heavy industry, from poverty to
prosperity, from inexperienced leaders to modern planners,
managers, and engineers.

4 Hong Kong and Singapore

HONG KONG AND SINGAPORE are commonly included as two of the four East Asian newly industrializing "countries," but they are in fact small city states that now serve as the centers of regions extending well beyond their borders. After World War II, as commercial networks expanded to cover a broader geographical area, each began functioning as its region's de facto capital for industry, finance, commerce, information, education, and culture—that is, as the center in all spheres except the political. Hong Kong's region includes parts of Southeast Asia and, since the opening of China in the 1970s, parts of southern China. Singapore's extends to nearby ASEAN countries, especially Malaysia and Indonesia.

As major world ports for over a century, Hong Kong and Singapore had a solid base in finance, shipping, insurance, information, and other services before they turned to industry after World War II. Both had a British colonial heritage and a familiarity with the English language and Western culture that gave them a great advantage over other East Asian locations in international commerce.

In the 1950s and 1960s, both had an agriculture sector consisting of rural truck farmers who brought their produce into the cities to sell. In the 1970s and 1980s, as the urban districts

grew and expanded, the rural areas were transformed into suburbs and linked by improved systems of transportation that
brought the whole metropolitan area within commuting range
of the city center. Farming virtually disappeared, and agricultural produce was imported from across the city states' political borders. For Hong Kong, the agricultural hinterland
became the Pearl River Delta area of China's Guangdong Province, and for Singapore, it became Malaysia. Unlike Japan,
South Korea, and Taiwan, the two city states thus had no
rural base within their borders to earn foreign currency and
provide savings that could be invested in industry.

Industrial transformation began in Hong Kong in the 1950s
and in Singapore in the 1960s. The populations of the two
city states were so small that their local consumer markets
could not serve as a base for local industries to build up
economies of scale before attempting to compete in world
markets. Even in 1990, Hong Kong had less than six million
people and Singapore less than three million. The small size of
their local markets led to an industrial strategy different from
that of Japan, Taiwan, and South Korea. There was no point
in using restrictive tariffs to protect their so-called infant industries. Nor could local industry come close to producing the
variety of products the local population needed and wanted
once personal incomes began to rise. The city states had no
choice but to concentrate industry in a small number of sectors
that could from the beginning produce goods on a scale large
enough to compete in the world market.

In all these ways, Hong Kong and Singapore had striking
similarities. And yet the approaches of the two cities to industrialization were in some ways almost polar opposites. Hong
Kong remained a British colony and had the most laissez-
faire approach to economic development of any of the little
dragons. Singapore, by contrast, became independent in 1965
and had a government that played the most activist role of the

little dragons, not only in guiding economic development but in managing enterprises and in shaping social development.

HONG KONG

Among industrialized economies, Hong Kong is perhaps the world's greatest anomoly. It is the only industrialized colony in existence, but, if anything, the neocolonial economic structure has come to work in reverse. By 1990 the average per capita income in Hong Kong was approaching that of its colonial motherland, England, and more investment was then flowing from the colony to the motherland than from the motherland to the colony. Hong Kong is an unusual colony in other respects as well. Ninety-eight percent of the population is ethnically Chinese, but there are now strong popular protests bemoaning the forthcoming British departure from Hong Kong and the resumption of Chinese sovereignty in 1997.

Initial industrialization in Hong Kong was prompted not so much by government strategy or by the efforts of local industrialists but by events beyond Hong Kong's control. Until 1950, the basic source of the city's economic vitality had been its entrepôt trade with China and the rest of the world. But as the Korean War began and the United States sealed the border to Communist China, this trade dried up. Among the refugees arriving from the mainland, however, were talented people who helped build a new economic base.

A small group of refugees from Shanghai who had been owners or managers of textile factories had escaped China with little capital or assets, but with their managerial skills fully intact. They arrived to find that Hong Kong banks were urgently seeking new ventures to replace the declining entrepôt trade. With local financing, therefore, they built factories in Tsuen Wan, along the southwest coast of Hong Kong's New

Territories, and immediately began producing low-cost products for world markets.[1]

Most of the refugees had limited entrepreneurial experience and little formal education. But they too proved to be a resource for industrialization. Many of them came from rural Guangdong, an area that had long been highly commercialized and responsive to international trade. Some of these refugees provided a willing source of cheap labor, and others were prepared to start small and middle-sized enterprises, both commercial and industrial.

The Government Approach to Industrialization

Many economists point enthusiastically to Hong Kong as an example of how success comes to free-market economies. Hong Kong's success, however, was aided by the government, whose civil servants greatly facilitated industrial planning and the development of local industry.

From 1949 on, Hong Kong's political stability rested on an unspoken agreement between Britain and China. The British and Hong Kong governments scrupulously avoided actions that might provoke the Chinese government, which had the military power to overrun Hong Kong if it chose. The Chinese in turn were willing to allow Hong Kong independence until 1997, and in 1984 decided to allow it to keep its capitalist system and a measure of autonomy for an additional fifty years beyond 1997. Hong Kong had proved to be a critical resource for China in its quest to earn foreign currency, acquire technology, and gain information about international business, and Hong Kong's success at industrializing only increased its value to China.

The colonial government in Hong Kong benefited from the closing of other British colonies and the winding down of the colonial service, which brought some of the service's most talented officers to the remaining colony. British civil servants in Hong Kong can be given high marks for their overall ability, for their training in the local Cantonese dialect, for the understanding of local circumstances they acquired as young district officers in the New Territories, for their integrity and resourcefulness, and for their commitment to Hong Kong. Hong Kong's locally recruited civil servants were also talented. Just as the civil service in Japan, Korea, and Taiwan drew the best graduates from Tokyo, Seoul National, and Taiwan universities so did Hong Kong's bureaucracy draw the top graduates of Hong Kong University, which had long provided excellent training for local youth.

The colonial government achieved a measure of insulation from short-range political pressures after 1949 because so many residents, including many emigrés from China, appreciated the commercial opportunities Hong Kong offered that were not available in China. Even many who grumbled about the colonial government pragmatically accepted British rule in order to avoid the risk of Communist takeover. Government officials selected prominent members of the Chinese community to serve on Hong Kong's Legislative Council and Executive Council. Although hardly democratically selected, these public representatives were respected within the community, and the system ensured a certain sensitivity on the part of government officials to local wishes. As Hong Kong's success widened the gap with the other side of the border, the preference of the city state's residents for Hong Kong over China grew stronger, thus increasing de facto support for the local government.

Historically, British civil servants did not play a leadership role in the industrialization and economic modernization of their nation's colonies. In Hong Kong, however, there had always been a close relationship between government officials and representatives of the Hong Kong branches of the largest

British commercial houses, such as Jardine Matheson and Butterfield and Swire, and this relationship continued as Hong Kong industrialized. Well represented on the Executive Council and the Legislative Council, the commercial houses kept the government attuned to the interests of business. In addition, because they had served as district officers and worked closely with local Chinese businesses, civil servants appreciated the needs of local enterprise. They also responded quickly to the needs of multinational companies from other countries, particularly the United States and Japan, that sought to establish regional office headquarters in Hong Kong.

In the 1950s and 1960s the Hong Kong government was fiscally conservative, and improvement of the infrastructure lagged behind the city's needs. After a disastrous fire broke out in squatter housing in 1953, the government gradually took responsibility for building a substantial amount of public housing, and by the 1970s and 1980s the government sped up the construction of roads, railways, ports, tunnels, a subway system, and an airport. It also moved to provide basic education for its growing population. Being smaller than Taiwan and South Korea, Hong Kong had more modest ambitions regarding the establishment of research institutes and engineering schools, but by the late 1980s, even with its small base, it began planning a university specializing in science and technology.

Although Hong Kong government officials extolled the operation of the free market and were less involved in guiding industrial development than their counterparts in the other little dragons, they did have a de facto industrial policy. They used public funds to develop many areas as industrial estates and then made the land available to manufacturing firms. For certain types of manufacturing firms that employed large numbers of people in key sectors, the government made land available at prices below market value. The colony's leadership also helped with export promotion and represented the position of local textile firms in international textile negotiations. In the late 1970s, when it looked as though textiles, which remained by far the largest sector in Hong Kong manufacturing, would have difficulty expanding in international markets, the government convened a commission to help promote diversification of industry. The government did not give direct aid to firms, but it helped focus attention on the problem and facilitated private sector initiatives. Perhaps even more important than any of these specific policies, however, was the government's success in maintaining social order, in providing a predictable rule of law free of corruption, and in responding to the needs of individual firms.

Entrepreneurs

If Hong Kong's government functioned in the background while industrialization took place, its entrepreneurs, by contrast, were visibly at the forefront. Prior to 1949, Hong Kong had handicraft industries that made carved ivory products, camphor chests, Chinese furniture, jade jewelry, and tailor-made apparel, but it had essentially no manufacturing. The first manufacturing breakthrough, in textile production, came in the early 1950s with the arrival of the Shanghai industrialists. The development of textile manufacturing also helped drive the expansion of the apparel industry. Other small entrepreneurs then moved into other labor-intensive industries, such as toys, plastic products, watches, and low-grade electronics.

As they became successful, Hong Kong business owners, like those in South Korea and Taiwan, sent their children abroad, mostly to England and North America, for higher education. The offspring who returned from overseas, trained in business management, finance, and engineering, were able to help their families' businesses branch out, upgrade technology, and deal with the subtleties of the international markets. Particularly in the 1970s and 1980s, Hong Kong firms diversified into higher-grade electronic products and improved the quality of their trade and international financial activities.

Yet Hong Kong, until the 1990s, was too small to develop its own engineering and science universities and gather a scientific community that could compare with what developed in Taiwan and South Korea. Hong Kong's great strength lay in finance and trade, and its industrialization benefited from these strengths. Even as their companies grew, Hong Kong's owner-entrepreneurs maintained tight control and kept well informed about international technology and markets. They justly prided themselves in their shrewd judgments and their ability to move more quickly than multinational executives, who were slowed by bureaucratic procedures.

After the reopening of the China market in the 1970s, Hong Kong had new opportunities to use its commercial skills as it resumed its traditional entrepôt role between mainland China and the world. As China moved away from socialist planning, small and medium-sized factories in Hong Kong that had begun to find local wages too high to remain competitive in world markets set up processing centers on the other side of the border. Such arrangements provided economic planners and entrepreneurs in South China with links to more advanced technology and world markets, and this in turn further energized Hong Kong.

TODAY, Hong Kong plays a larger role than ever before in shipping and in financial markets. Yet it was the development of manufacturing and light industry in Hong Kong that had made the crucial difference in saving the local economy when the bamboo curtain to China was closed. In the four decades from 1950 to 1990, Hong Kong business owners, far from interfering with industrial development, used their commercial and marketing skills to expand the international sales of Hong Kong products, thus strengthening their industry at home. Although Hong Kong residents constantly express worries about their future after China "resumes sovereignty" in 1997, Hong Kong remains a vibrant trading and financial center, not only for South China and Southeast Asia, but for the entire world.

SINGAPORE

Singapore has the most diverse population base of the little dragons and is the only new nation among them.[2] When Taiwan, South Korea, and Hong Kong sought political unity, they could draw on a long history based on strong ethnic identity. Singapore, by contrast, had to forge a new national identity with a population that was 75 percent Chinese, 15 percent Malay, and 7 percent Indian, each with its own language and tradition. And while the Chinese in Hong Kong were overwhelmingly Cantonese, the Chinese in Singapore were split into major groups who found each other's dialects unintelligible. In 1980, for example, there were 800,000 Fujianese, locally called Hokkien and in turn subdivided into the Amoy and the Fuzhou; 400,000 Chaozhouese, locally called Teochew; 300,000 Cantonese; 140,000 Hakka; and 130,000 Hainanese. The Chinese lingua franca became Mandarin, which is for Singaporeans a dialect learned in this generation and devoid of deep family-rooted ethnic significance. And because the city state was confronted by threatening neighbors who feared the potential linkage between local Chinese and China, Singapore played down its Chinese identity. Indeed, in 1963 Singapore's leaders, concerned about national security after the British left, chose to be part of Malaysia. Malaysia, however, was sufficiently worried that the strength of Singapore and its Chinese population would dominate the Malays that it cast Singapore aside, forcing it to be independent. Even after 1965, to maintain good relations with Malaysia, Singapore retained Malay as the city's official language, but by the 1980s the two dominant languages were English and Mandarin Chinese. Only in the late 1980s, as Malaysia and Indonesia became less fearful of Chinese ethnic dominance and as Indonesia normalized relations with China, could Singaporeans afford to begin openly stressing their Chinese identity.

During Japan's occupation of Taiwan and Korea, Japanese power was strong enough to prevent an anticolonial movement, and colonization ended suddenly with Japan's defeat. In Hong Kong, refugees from China were hardly interested in an anticolonial movement. To the extent that the Singapore government had a political history, however, it lay in its anticolonial struggle against Great Britain. Some of Singapore's post-independence leaders had first joined the anticolonial movement in England, where anticolonialism was closely linked with socialism, and at a time when socialist governments and the nationalization of key industries in Europe were at their peak. After Singapore became independent, these leaders made social policy more central to their aims than was true of leaders of the other little dragons. Although Prime Minister Lee Kuan-yew and his allies split with the more radical left after independence, they continued to believe in the desirability of government-led enterprises and the responsibility of the government for social security, housing, and medical care. Singapore was thus a striking contrast to Hong Kong's free-market capitalism. How did Singapore achieve political unity without drawing on ethnic identity, and how did it develop the efficiency needed to compete in international markets without giving up state responsibility for social welfare?

The Achievement of Unity and the Government's Approach to Industrialization

Singapore had a great advantage in being the only little dragon with a genuinely charismatic leader. Lee Kuan-yew had proved himself courageous and resolute both in Singapore's struggle against colonialism and the Communists and in its confrontation with Indonesia. As he skillfully guided Singapore through its difficult early years, he acquired a stature that gave him enormous leeway in shaping Singapore's course. He also excelled as a technocrat and, fortunately for Singapore, he had both the political skill to forge alliances that enabled him to remain in office over a quarter of a century and the overall vision necessary to set Singapore on a solid path of progress.

In Japan, Taiwan, and South Korea, as the role of the politician began to be differentiated from that of the bureaucrat, meritocratic exams continued to be used for selecting bureaucrats, but not for selecting politicians. Japan had career politicians, and Korea and Taiwan had politicians who came from the military officers' corps. In Singapore, Lee and his right-hand man, Goh Keng-swee, were such believers in meritocracy that they even selected political candidates for their Political Action Party from those who had been the most outstanding as university students. Rationality, legal procedures, and meritocracy played a larger role in the making of public policy in Singapore than elsewhere.

In Japan and the other three little dragons, political decisions have long been made behind the scenes by officials maneuvering to forge a consensus among the inner circles. In Singapore, the city's first generation of leaders had been well trained by the British in the art of rhetoric, and Lee Kuan-yew and other officials relished public debate. A highly articulate public debating style, which made Singapore's political culture unique within East Asia, could be permitted because Lee Kuan-yew had a secure base. Lee so dominated politics and achieved such a broad basis of public support that as Chan Heng-chee, later ambassador to the United Nations, put it, in Singapore, "politics disappeared" and Singapore became an "administrative state." [3]

With a population of less than three million people, Singapore had a small circle of politicians and bureaucrats who were in close contact with each other during the period of industrialization. The bureaucrats concerned with the economy held a wide variety of positions and often changed posts over the years, but the key economic bureaucrats formed a small coherent group under the leadership of Goh Keng-swee. Singapore's initial economic plans after independence drew heavily on the United Nations Study Group report drawn up under the direction of Albert Winsemius, a Dutch economist. But the strategy for and the implementation of Singapore's industrial development was firmly in the hands of the Economic Development Board, established in 1961.

As Singapore began its industrialization drive in the early 1960s, Lee Kuan-yew and Goh Keng-swee were convinced that the local business community, consisting overwhelmingly of small merchants and financiers, did not possess either the skills in technology and management or the commitment to the public good needed to guide the industrialization process. From the outset, therefore, unlike Japan and the other little dragons, they tried to attract multinational corporations and to establish their own corporations that were managed directly or indirectly by the government.

To induce multinational companies to invest in Singapore, leaders permitted a level of foreign control that Taiwan and South Korea, more confident of their own entrepreneurial talent, would have found unacceptable. Singapore wanted the multinationals not only because they provided high levels of technology and management skill but because they ensured access to world markets that Singapore, as a small player, without Hong Kong's cosmopolitan entrepreneurs, would have trouble penetrating alone. The government did, however, retain regulatory powers it used to ensure that the companies that came to Singapore remained good corporate citizens.

Singapore leaders also took great care in selecting the foreign companies whose investment they approved. They sought stable corporations that had advanced technology and were prepared to invest for the long term. In 1961 Singapore boldly began constructing its first large industrial park in Jurong, which was soon filled with acceptable multinationals, and other industrial parks followed. It attracted companies such as General Electric, Hewlett Packard, NEC, and Fujitsu, not primarily because of tax and investment incentives, but because the government was stable and efficient and because it had done a good job of training and disciplining its workers. At the time of independence, literacy levels in Singapore lagged behind those of the other three dragons, but the government moved quickly to raise standards of education. In addition, officials, convinced of the value of the opportunity to upgrade their labor force, happily supplied special training programs to meet the labor needs of the multinationals. The government was pleased to provide skilled workers and infrastructure to encourage multinational managers to make products such as disk drives, which enjoyed a small niche in the world market but which Singapore could produce competitively on a mass scale.

The Singapore government invested directly in a substantial number of ventures and sometimes assigned regular civil servants to serve as managers. Since the bureaucracy drew the very top students from the universities, those who went into the private sector directly after their schooling rarely had distinguished academic records. During the colonial period, those who had performed best in school exams were admitted to

Singapore's elite school, Raffles, and then went to England for further training, with the expectation that they would return and serve the government. Lee Kuan-yew and Goh Keng-swee had been among the most talented of this group. There was no commercial or technical training route that attracted comparable talent. And yet in Singapore, as in Hong Kong, the entire climate had already been so commercialized that even government bureaucrats were infused with commercial acumen and a powerful commitment to efficiency and performance. In a very real sense, the leading business entrepreneurs in Singapore are government bureaucrats. In government-run businesses, the promotion of officials depended on the profitability of the operations they guided. Government-owned enterprises that were not profitable, such as printing plants, were reorganized or abandoned. "We have," as one Singapore leader aptly put it, "capitalism with socialist characteristics."

To generate capital for industrial development, the government established a Central Provident Fund with resources generated from wages. At its peak, the Central Provident Fund took some 50 percent of all wages, half from the employer and half from the employee; Singapore thereby achieved the highest savings rate in the world. Funds were used to finance the development of industry, transportation and communications, infrastructure, parks, and housing. Keeping up their socialist heritage, Singapore leaders built over 80 percent of the city's housing with public funds. The money paid to the Central Provident Fund from wages was listed in the name of the employee, and the employee could draw on this fund to secure housing mortgages as well as to meet medical, retirement, and other selected welfare needs. The result was a very high percentage of home ownership, arguably the best average housing stock in Asia, and a relatively satisfied work force that identified with stable middle-class values. Neither personal security nor Singapore's overall security, moreover, was linked to a particular firm, which also contributed to a solid base of national community stability that elsewhere is supplied by ethnic identity and political history.

In the late 1970s, Singapore's leaders, frightened by the prospect that China, with its infinite supply of cheap labor, might begin exporting industrial products, sought ways to hasten Singapore's development of higher technology. Unhappy that companies paying low wages did not feel under pressure to introduce more efficient machinery, from 1979 to 1981 the government pushed through substantial wage raises. High wages, although they made some Singapore goods less competitive in international markets and thus contributed, along with the decrease in oil exploration and shipbuilding, to the economic downturn in the mid-1980s, allowed Singapore to accelerate its transition to higher technology in the late 1980s.

Entrepreneurs: Public and Multinational

When the government began its industrial development program in the 1960s, Singapore had only a limited number of small manufacturing establishments in food processing, beverages, and printing. The multinationals attracted to Singapore were largely in electronics and machinery, areas that could profitably employ workers who already enjoyed wages that were on the average higher than in the other little dragons.

With its funds from the Central Provident Fund, the Singapore government not only provided infrastructure for multinational companies but, in certain key sectors, developed its own state companies. One sector included petroleum refining, petrochemical products, and oil exploration equipment, a field in which Singapore could take advantage of the development of the nearby Indonesian oil fields. To capitalize on its position as an important port on international shipping routes between Japan and the Middle East, Singapore also established government shipbuilding and ship repair facilities. Officials realized that Singapore was too small to attempt to develop such industries completely on its own, and they therefore formed alliances with U.S. companies in the oil industry and with Japanese companies in shipbuilding.

In companies managed or funded by the government, Singapore experimented with a wide variety of funding mechanisms but kept the ultimate control in government hands. Talented civil servants served as long as necessary in companies' executive positions. The government had no objection to the growth of small local businesses, as well; and many of them did expand, especially those in commerce, banking, and other service areas, but these independent businesses play a smaller role in Singapore than in the other little dragons. Because multinationals and government firms dominated the early decades of industrialization, the spirit of Singapore's enterprises has been more like that of the mature large modern corporation than has been true in the other little dragons, where the early decades of industrialization were dominated by the free-swinging first-generation founders of family firms. In both multinational and government-led industries in Singapore, professional managers were trained through special programs and promoted on a regular and predictable basis. Fewer personal fortunes were made in Singapore. Singapore's success came less from the raw energy of individual enterprise and more from the deliberate planning of bureaucratic managers and multinational executives. Singapore thus made a striking contrast to Hong Kong, where the government played a smaller role and individual entrepreneurs a far larger role. Hong Kong's industrialization was more volatile and personal, Singapore's more orderly and predictable. If Hong Kong entrepreneurs thought of Singapore as a bit dull, rigid, and too tightly controlled,

Singapore's leaders thought of Hong Kong as too speculative, decadent, and undisciplined. Singapore's leaders were proud that they could provide their citizens on the average with a slightly higher income and substantially better living quarters than were available to citizens of the other little dragons.

IN SHORT, Singapore's industrialization involved a peculiar blend: a charismatic national leader, meritocratic politicians, bureaucrats skilled in public debate, capitalist entrepreneurs who were government bureaucrats, a substantial welfare program on a sound financial basis, and foreign managers. And yet even Singapore, in many ways the most distinctive of the little dragons, had many features common to the other three and to Japan.

5 Toward an Explanation

WHAT COMMON features found in these societies on the East Asian periphery—Japan, South Korea, Taiwan, Hong Kong, and Singapore—explain why they made the industrial breakthrough while others did not? Now that it is apparent that Japan and the four little dragons have completed their process of transformation into industrialized societies, it is appropriate to address this underlying issue—to reflect on the nature of this unique period in East Asia, and also to consider how the achievements of this era are affecting the entire world.

Because all five of these societies share a Confucian heritage, intellectuals who admire the East Asian tradition find appealing the notion that the key to success lies in Confucianism. In addition, Western social scientists influenced by Max Weber are captivated by the intriguing parallel between a Protestant ethic that helped spawn Western capitalism and a Confucian ethic that helped breed East Asian industrialization.[1]

The argument, however, deserves a tough-minded examination and requires, at a minimum, some important qualifications. Many countries have achieved an industrial transformation without Confucianism; and other countries without such a heritage, such as Malaysia, Thailand, Turkey, Brazil, and

Mexico, may succeed in industrializing by the early years of the twenty-first century.[2] Will we then glorify the Latin American Catholic or the Moslem reform tradition, and if we do, will not the concept of "tradition," encompassing so many diverse heritages, lose its explanatory power?

We must also recall from the late 1940s and the 1950s the many arguments, not entirely without foundation, that the Confucian heritage retarded modernization and left East Asian nations far behind the West.[3]

Furthermore, the heartland of Confucianism, mainland China, has not yet achieved industrial transformation. If Confucianism alone explains why countries modernize, why should the Confucian motherland lag behind? It is true that after 1949, failure can be attributed to socialist planning, but China had not achieved widespread industrialization before 1949, either.

And within East Asia, the breakthroughs in industrialization have occurred not in the great centers of Confucian faith or among the groups most imbued with Confucianism. If anything, just as Max Weber found that the greatest drive to industrialize in his time came in areas located far from Catholic orthodoxy, so in East Asia industrialization prospered in areas far from the centers of traditional Confucian orthodoxy, where trade and commerce were most highly developed. And successes occurred not under the old Confucian-style governments but in societies that had cast them aside for new governments, with very different political systems.

These points do not entirely discredit arguments about Confucianism, to which I will return, but they require us to give full consideration to situational factors that helped East Asian countries respond effectively to the post-war opportunities for industrialization.

Situational Factors

Among East Asia's situational advantages for industrializing after World War II were the following.

U.S. Aid   East Asian nations received massive aid from the United States and from international organizations, which gave them extensive opportunities for contact with knowledgeable foreigners. These were overwhelmingly Americans, who became in effect tutors, not only in modern technology and management, but in the broader aspects of industrial society.[4] Because American advisors could provide East Asians with appropriate advice and training of greater depth than any textbook could transmit, they were perhaps even more crucial than the financial, military, and technical aid. Hundreds of thousands of Americans were stationed in Japan during the Allied occupation from 1945 to 1952; and throughout the Cold War, the United States offered technical advice and assistance in nearly every sphere of life to Japan, Taiwan, and South Korea. After 1945, because the United States and its allies fought two major wars in Asia, in Korea and Vietnam, and because East Asian countries were in the front line of the battle against communism, Americans made a higher level of commitment to East Asia than to any other area except Western Europe.

Although Hong Kong and Singapore received less direct American aid, they, like Japan and the other little dragons, benefited from the stimulus their economies received in offering rear services to the allied troops during the Korean and Vietnam wars. The Japanese economy, from 1950 on, not only received a great overall boost from the "special procurement" of the Korean War, but also gained expertise in advanced technology and management systems needed to coordinate support services and repair equipment. In the Vietnam War, similar advantages accrued to all the economies in the region and were particularly important for South Korea's construction industry.

Destruction of the Old Order   Japanese colonial conquest and war destroyed the conservative political order in East Asia that might have resisted adaptation to new realities. Before the end of the nineteenth century, the conservative Confucian order in Korea and China, including Taiwan, was presided over by governments poorly adapted to guiding industrial modernization. Disdain for physical labor, a contempt for merchants and restraints on their activities, the base of support among rural elites who resisted land reform, and the conservative application of Confucian teachings all impeded the introduction of newer ways of thinking.

Japan's colonial expansion into Taiwan and Korea and later its invasion of Hong Kong and Singapore undermined the social and economic basis of the old Confucian order. After World War II, the old rural social base was ended in South Korea and Taiwan by land reform, and in Hong Kong and Singapore by urban expansion that replaced rural areas with suburbs. In Hong Kong and Singapore, although Britain resumed its sovereignty after the war, the defeat of the British forces by the Japanese in 1941 destroyed the seemingly invincible aura of Westerners. Neither the British nor their local supporters were ever able to recapture the mystique they had previously enjoyed in the two city states.

The new governments established after World War II in Japan and in the little dragons were less beholden to the traditional elites and were therefore freer to make policy decisions without considering their interests. The military power of the mainlanders who suppressed Taiwanese opposition in 1947 and of Park Chung Hee, who led a coup in Korea in 1961, gave these governments great independence from local pressure groups. In Singapore, Lee Kuan-yew, as a charismatic hero of the early anticolonial struggles, was not beholden to the local business community; and in Hong Kong, British rulers were not controlled by the local business elite. These new governments were thus able to develop what Stephan Haggard and other political scientists have described as a "strong state," relatively insulated from local elites.[5] Taiwan and South Korea, in particular, were able to undertake land reform, thereby further undermining the power base of the traditional rural elite. Social networks and *guanxi* (purposively cultivated personal relationships) remained important, but they were weakened, and a subtle but fundamental shift occurred in the way they were used. The desire for economic achievement had become so powerful that leaders used the networks to accomplish new goals more than local supporters used the networks to gain access to leaders to divide the spoils of power.[6]

Sense of Political and Economic Urgency   East Asia became imbued with a sense of both political and economic urgency that helped mobilize local support for industrial development. Japan and the four little dragons each perceived themselves to be under a continuing military threat, and the lesson of World War II, that America won because of its superior economic base, was well understood. By the 1960s, with the prospect that America would wind down its aid to East Asia, both military and economic, leaders in these countries were convinced that to defend themselves they had to acquire a strong industrial base in order to buy or, preferably, to make the equipment they needed.

The sense of urgency in these five states also derived from economic realities. With increased populations after World War II and limited geographic area and resources, they had little hope of becoming self-sufficient in food and raw materials. They believed they had to export manufactured goods in order to pay for the imports of food and raw materials that they needed to survive.

These fears created a climate in which many leaders were prepared to work together to resolve their internal differences. The fears also created among the general public a willingness to endure short-term economic sacrifices. It is easy to imagine that political order and high savings rates might have been achieved by governments without the assaults on individual life, liberty, and dignity that occurred in many instances in the early era of industrial breakthrough in all these societies. But the fact is that these authoritarian governments did keep order and provided policies conducive to growth, and that the sense of military and economic urgency helped reinforce the willingness of the public to accept that order. The governments could follow policies that constrained private spending, increased investment, kept funds at home, and channeled the investment into areas conducive to growth.

The governments used both sticks and carrots to discourage business owners from taking their assets abroad. Japan, South Korea, and Taiwan placed strict limits on the export of capital in the early years, when there was a constant shortage of capital for local investments. But the governments also played a critical role in providing incentives and security for businesses, both local and foreign, to channel funds from abroad and from local savings into investment for industry and infrastructure.

Eager and Plentiful Labor Force   Japan and the four little dragons had available a new labor force, eager to work and improve its skills to meet the needs of industry. By the time industrialization began, each of these societies had a large dislocated population that was anxious to find a new basis of economic livelihood. In Japan, six million soldiers and civilians had returned in the late 1940s from the overseas posts where they had served Japan's colonial and military expansion. In Taiwan over one and a half million people had fled from mainland China by the early 1950s; and by the end of the Korean War, over two million North Koreans had fled to the South.

In Hong Kong, after the closing of the Chinese border in 1950, refugees from China constituted over half the population; and in Singapore a substantial portion of the population had immigrated from Malaysia and Indonesia.

Elite groups in all these societies were uprooted by the turmoil and institutional changes. In Japan, the samurai class had been terminated in the 1870s and military officers were retired from service in 1945. In the three little dragons where colonialism had ended, those serving the colonialists found their positions gone when colonialism ended. These displaced members of the elite, accustomed to leadership, eagerly sought and often found appropriate new opportunities. Under the new structure of the government and the economy, with new flexibility, many of them gained fresh perspectives and grew with the new challenges. These individuals provided a coherent core of creative leadership in new organizations.

In Japan, Taiwan, and South Korea, moreover, during the early years of industrialization, large numbers of workers migrated from the countryside to the towns and cities, eagerly seeking jobs in industry. Mechanization in agriculture, particularly the use of small hand tractors, meant that fewer rural workers were needed than before, and the pressures of overpopulation led them to pursue new opportunities in urban areas.

In all these societies, as a result of war and the division of land ownership, traditional property ownership was, in the early years of industrialization, no longer a major means of gaining wealth and prestige. Workers and their families wanted not only wages but skills and careers that would give them the long-range security that small parcels of land, at that point, could not provide. Later, by the 1980s, as massive urban migration and acute urban land shortage escalated the cost of land, real estate reemerged as an important source of wealth. But most of the population relied on their own skills and labor as their major source of income.

Because they were so poor, many workers accepted industrial jobs that required physical exertion and offered, by international standards, relatively low wages. Although labor shortages began to develop by the 1980s, in the early decades of industrialization there were far more workers than jobs, which meant that would-be workers competed even for low-wage industrial employment.

The Japanese Model The four little dragons had available the Japanese model and Japanese technology and investment. Although a Confucian nation, Japan, as an island over a hundred miles from the Asian mainland, had by the seventeenth century developed its own feudal system, with clans that had a measure of local autonomy administered by samurai-bureaucrats who were not landholders. Hence, in the latter part of the nineteenth century, when Japanese leaders used the fear of foreign encroachment to launch the Meiji Restoration, these samurai-bureaucrats were less resistant to change and to learning from Europe and North America than the landholding elite in many other countries.[7]

After World War II, the Japanese model was of great importance to Taiwan, South Korea, Hong Kong, and Singapore. The four little dragons shared with Japan a substantial heritage, including a written language that used Chinese characters. The geographical closeness of Japan and the history of commercial relations before World War II, furthermore, made Japan more accessible for them than it was for more distant economies.

These four societies also had many other circumstances similar to Japan's. Like Japan, they were densely populated and short on natural resources. They had to export to obtain food and resources. In part because of migration, they like Japan initially had a relatively young population, with many young people entering the labor force each year. These new employees had relatively high levels of literacy, making them a highly teachable work force; and in school students had developed an acute awareness of how much they lagged behind Europe and North America.

South Korea and Taiwan had the broadest base for understanding Japan because of the length of their Japanese occupation. Hong Kong and Singapore, however, had been headquarters for large numbers of Japanese troops and their civilian Japanese supporters, who left a very strong impact. With this forced intimate contact, all four societies had a basic understanding of Japan's pattern of industrialization.

After World War II, only the governments of South Korea and Singapore consciously studied the Japanese experience in detail, but the main outlines of the Japanese strategy were well understood by all four of the little dragons. They all knew that Japan began with labor-intensive industries and used the income from exports in this sector to purchase new equipment, while upgrading its training and technology in sectors where productivity gains would allow higher wages. They all saw the crucial role of government in guiding these changes. Having the Japanese model provided both the confidence that they too could succeed and a perspective on how to proceed.

As Japanese wages began to rise and Japanese allowed some factories in labor-intensive sectors to move off shore, the geographic closeness and the history of commercial contacts with these other East Asian nations made it easier for Japanese companies to set up factories in them rather than elsewhere in the world.

These five situational factors—U.S. aid, the destruction of the old order, a sense of political and economic urgency, an eager and plentiful labor force, and familiarity with the Japanese model of success—came together to give a powerful advantage to East Asian countries. Although some societies outside East Asia shared some of these factors, none of them came close to East Asia in combining so many of them.

Industrial Neo-Confucianism

With such favorable situational factors for industrialization, why must one consider tradition at all? The answer, in brief, is that situational factors alone do not account for all that happened. Above all, industrialization requires high levels of coordination, precise timing, and predictability. To break into industrial competition in the middle of the twentieth century required even higher levels of coordination and teamwork, deeper understanding of science, technology, and management skills, and far greater knowledge of world markets than in earlier eras. The little dragons' success in industrializing cannot be explained by their situation alone. One must ask what it was that gave the present generation the ability to achieve the needed complex levels of organization; and this achievement cannot be separated from the institutional practices and underlying attitudes, what Robert Bellah and others call the "habits of the heart," that they absorbed in growing up in their culture.

Amid all the rapid changes in East Asia—material, spiritual, and organizational—these traditional factors are not easy to identify. I have selected four clusters of institutions and traditional attitudes, common to all these societies, that with some adaptations I believe contributed to the capacity of Japan and the four little dragons to industrialize. There is no simple objective scientific formula for identifying these clusters. Other observers would produce different lists; and a researcher can only examine contemporary institutions, compare them with some of the "traditional" ones that existed before the great transformations,[8] and study how the institutions have evolved in the interim. In each of these four clusters, I will consider not only the traditional institutions but also the new hybrid forms that developed in the course of industrialization to adapt to new circumstances.[9]

Meritocratic Elite The development of a meritocratically selected bureaucracy was one of the great contributions of East Asia to world civilization. Although, as Max Weber noted, all modern societies make use of bureaucracies, there are still some significant enduring differences between bureaucracy in the West and in East Asia. In his discussion of how bureaucracy brings rational rule to modern society, Weber distinguished the role of the bureaucrat, who provides technocratic expertise, from that of the politician, who makes policy. Yet this distinction, common in modern Western governments, was not one that played a major role in the Confucian tradition. In Confucian societies, the bureaucrat had a broader responsibility than in the West, and enjoyed more authority and respect than his Western counterparts.

The Confucian bureaucrat, selected on the basis of merit, had a sense of responsibility for the overall social order, including the overall moral tone of the society. The guidelines for proper exercise of his role gave less attention to the technical rules for his position than in many Western societies and more attention to how his behavior and decisions affected the moral order.

Confucian society was unabashedly elitist, and Confucian thought was less concerned than Western theory with how to structure restraints on the power of the leaders. It was not expected that the masses would exercise sovereignty over the government or even over the selection of the leaders. Elite Confucian bureaucrats were also less constrained by legal precedent. The top official could change rules by new decrees, and a local official was in effect a judge as well as an administrator.

In the post-war period, as in earlier times, bureaucrats in East Asian countries have a very important role in decision making, are selected in a meritocratic manner, have a sense of responsibility for the overall welfare of society, and until recently, have functioned under relatively few constraints from politicians or the masses.

As democracy expanded after World War II, elected politicians came to have meaningful power, first in Japan and later in Singapore, Taiwan, and South Korea. But even when top officials were elected directly, bureaucrats still played a large role in making decisions on important issues.

Although there was thus great continuity in the meritocratic selection of the bureaucrat, in his elitist position and in his insulation from pressure from the masses, in the twentieth century other aspects of the bureaucrat's role underwent great changes. In Japan these changes began gradually in the middle of the Meiji period, but in the four little dragons they were introduced more suddenly, after World War II. The role of the bureaucrat became increasingly specialized, and within each specialty, bureaucrats became well informed about how Western bureaucrats performed similar roles. East Asian bureaucrats began to see the course of history not as cyclical but as progressive, and they began to measure their success by their contribution to their society's economic and technological advancement. A far larger proportion of them specialized in economic matters than ever before.

In earlier periods of history, bureaucrats tended to be suspicious of private economic development and feared that too much private accumulation of wealth could undermine their political power. As modern bureaucrats became aware of Western economic progress, they came to believe not only that economic vitality came from the private sector, but that the government could develop new ways to keep a measure of control while giving private enterprises vastly more independence, and that their proper government role was to help the private sector prosper. Even in Singapore, where the old attitude of moral disdain toward the merchant perhaps remained strongest, multinational companies were given considerable leeway and government-financed companies were expected to behave like private profit-maximizing corporations.

The bureaucratic system, in its modern form, played a critical role in industrialization. Some of the ablest people in the society were chosen, and they were given broad-gauged training and experience in many different positions before being assigned major responsibilities. On the whole they remained dedicated to overall public goals and, while provided a measure of guaranteed benefits, exercised restraint in their private pursuit of wealth. The fact that they were selected by meritocratic measures, were reputed to be highly moral, and lived without conspicuous display gave them an unquestioned legitimacy that encouraged public compliance with their decisions and thus helped to provide a stable base of support for their governments. Meritocratic selection gave a substantial measure of legitimacy to governments that would be regarded as authoritarian in the West,[10] where the public is believed to have greater rights and no government is granted legitimacy unless officials are selected by public voting.

Concern for the overall social order led officials to be sensitive to problems of inequality early in the process of industrialization and to make efforts to spread income opportunities to all parts of society. At the same time, bureaucrats in these societies were always strict in handling deviants and were not as concerned as Westerners about individual rights when questions of overall social order seemed at stake. Japan and the four little dragons have achieved very tight control over crime. Unlike bureaucrats in most Western nations, higher-level East Asian bureaucrats have been given considerable discretion and have been judged less by their performance of specific role assignments and more by how well the entire system has maintained social order and advanced along the path to economic prosperity. Westerners would not be comfortable with many aspects of this system, but it is hard to deny that this modern form of meritocratic bureaucracy contributed greatly to East Asia's industrial transformation.

Entrance Exam System   Exams remain the crucial gateway to prestige and power. The traditional gateway to officialdom was through examinations that measured not basic intelligence or aptitude but the capacity to master certain material through long years of study. In many Western educational institutions, examinations are used to determine certification for completing a course of study. In East Asia, the critical examinations have always been at the entrance.

As East Asian nations began to industrialize, the content of examinations was fundamentally altered. Confucian teachings and stylized essays were replaced by demonstrated knowledge of foreign languages, modern history, economics, science, and mathematics. As in traditional times, success in examinations still required study and memorization.

Perhaps even more important than the change in content was the expanded use of exams. In the labor-intensive industries that characterized the early years of industrialization, low levels of skills were required, much of the employment was in relatively small family enterprises, and examinations were not necessary for the selection of new workers. But as more skills were required and work organizations grew in size, examinations came to be used on a much broader scale to select new employees. First-generation founders of businesses commonly acquired wealth and fame without passing examinations. Even they, however, made an effort to provide their children the best education possible and thus enable them to acquire the deeper respect that their societies accord to those who pass exams.

As basic education was improved to include the entire population, competition for the small number of attractive positions became even more intense than before. Students began preparing for exams at a younger age, and entrance examinations were used to select students for the better secondary and sometimes even elementary schools. The majority of young people in all these societies began to prepare for examinations in their early teens. They studied hard not only because of the value placed on learning itself but because of the specific link between entrance examinations and good jobs. During the period of rapid industrialization, young people attained good positions not through inheriting family land or property but through passing examinations. "Examination hell" became very real for most young East Asians, far more so on the average than for their counterparts in Europe and North America.

The importance of entrance examinations for gaining admission to the better schools and for acquiring the better jobs has created a whole set of practices that are strikingly similar in each of these societies. Teachers, school administrators, the students' families—and the students themselves—are oriented toward preparation for the next all-important examination. School systems are measured by the success of their graduates in passing examinations for the next higher level; and since success is so precisely measurable, parents of school children and higher officials in the national education bureaucracy keep pressure on each school to push it to higher standards.

As excruciating as examinations may be for those students and families who feel the competition most keenly, the system has had several advantages for a nation undertaking industrialization. The extension of the examination principle was critical in overcoming feudal favoritism. In all these societies, the use of personal connections and relationships had in an earlier era been important in selecting people for many important positions. Not only does personal favoritism make it impossible to enforce standards of performance in the workplace, but it makes it difficult for the mass of the population, excluded from any opportunity to get such positions, to accept the fairness of the system. By breaking down the importance of feudal connections of family and locality in placement, the exam system has allowed all members of the society to feel that they have access to high positions.

The structure of the examination and job placement systems also ensures that the most talented people in the society are trained and channeled into key positions in government and large corporations that will help advance the society as a whole. It ensures that people in these leadership positions have a broad understanding of historical forces and a solid base of knowledge. Perhaps most important, the examination system and the intense competition it generates ensure that young people will exert themselves to acquire the information and knowledge that will help them pass examinations. The exams are of sufficient difficulty that students, their teachers, and their parents realize that to pass them, long years of disciplined effort are required. The classroom thus encourages both learning and disciplined work habits, acquired over a number of years, that make students desirable employees at a later stage.

The Importance of the Group   Another cluster of Confucian attitudes, centering on the importance of the group over the individual, has also undergone significant modification. In the course of industrialization, perhaps no part of the Confucian core has been subjected to such criticism. Many leaders who studied Western progress came to believe that group attachment and loyalty inhibited rationality and the individual drive necessary for progress. Many young people, feeling burdened by the weight of group pressure, struck out at the shackles placed on their freedom. During the last several decades, some of the harshness of group demands constraining the individual and pressuring each person to sacrifice for the group have been lessened in all these societies.[11]

And yet many East Asians equate the Western emphasis on individualism with selfishness and egoism and still find it repugnant. They regard Western concern with human rights as excessive, the widespread use of drugs and the high crime rates in the West as a sign of undesirable permissiveness and decadence, and Westerners' seeming lack of concern for overall social order as disastrous.

But the nature of the groups to which one is loyal in East Asia has also changed. The importance of ascriptive groups such as the family and local community has declined, and the importance of new solidarities such as the place of employment and occupational specialty has grown, as have the extent and significance of different networks that go beyond one's own group, reaching even into the international community.[12]

East Asian societies even today do not place as much emphasis on binding legal codes as do societies in the West, but East Asia has traditionally had tightly structured societies with more detailed rules about the proper behavior of the individual in his or her group. These societies grant less room for the individual to behave in idiosyncratic ways. Group leaders not only teach these values but accept responsibility for members who abide by the rules of proper behavior and apply social pressure on those who do not.

The emphasis on group loyalty, the responsiveness of people in organizations to group demands, and the predictability of individual behavior in the group setting have been characteristics well suited to the needs of industrialization, especially for the late late developer, where centralized coordination has been so critical.

Many East Asians are convinced that some of the concepts and theories that Westerners think of as universal are culturally limited. Government officials concerned with economic matters, for example, consider Western economic theory that assumes that individuals are driven overwhelmingly by material incentives to be overdrawn. They are convinced, rather, that a desirable society gives more place to consideration of other people regardless of profit sheets and that individuals do respond to moral suasion and social pressures as well as to material rewards. Many leaders in these societies have tried to structure their economic organizations and their systems of social control accordingly. As Ronald Dore and others have pointed out, there is a difference between the Western stress on allocative efficiency, where the concern is to allocate resources to areas where they can bring the best return, and "production efficiency," where the concern is with the overall output and goal.[13] East Asians put less stress on allocative efficiency, but their concern with providing for group members who devote themselves to the group reinforces loyalty that, in the long run, may bring more efficiency even by Western standards.

Since the group to which someone belongs is a continuing one, attention to the group implies a time horizon beyond the immediate present. In the crucial early stages of industrialization, as incomes grew, people were willing to limit their personal consumption in order to save and invest in the future of their family or firm. And because the family and the local community accepted substantial responsibility for the welfare of their members, most individuals in the society had a safety net even before the government funded a substantial national welfare system. Meanwhile, the government could channel funds into industry and infrastructure.[14]

At the workplace, concern for the group helped create pliant workers, willing to accept a limited role for labor unions and yet ready to exert themselves for the firm without making great personal demands. These values tended to keep down protest movements that might have disrupted industrial production. Intellectuals and other observers, in East Asia and abroad, see the dark side of many of these practices, but if one focuses on the narrow question of their impact on rapid industrialization, it is hard to deny their contribution.

Self-cultivation   Self-cultivation is perhaps the closest analogue in Confucian culture to the Protestant work ethic in strengthening the personal drive for achievement. In Weber's analysis, Protestants believed in predestination for salvation, and some might have thought this would limit the individual's drive for achievement. But in fact people wanted to prove to themselves and to others that they were predestined for good and not for evil, and this impulse was channeled into productive work. For traditional followers of Confucianism, self-cultivation was driven by a desire for more perfect control over one's emotions and required study and reflection more than activism. Today one can still observe East Asians who privately pursue meditation or practice hobbies such as calligraphy, poetry writing, painting, or musical performance, where they continuously strive for composure and self-improvement.

Yet the drive for self-improvement can take an active purposive form, manifested in the effort to advance work-related skills such as speaking foreign languages, using computers, calculating statistics, and understanding foreign markets. In the office and factory, the drive can be channeled into continuous efforts to improve group performance by increasing product quality, market share, and international reputation. This restless desire for improvement, utilized by the firm, goes beyond short-term aims and material acquisition. It is possible that further affluence will eventually erode the impulse, but the will to improve has already outlasted the early stages of affluence.

THESE FOUR institutions and cultural practices rooted in the Confucian tradition but adapted to the needs of an industrial society—a meritocratic elite, an entrance exam system, the importance of the group, and the goal of self-improvement—have helped East Asia make use of their special situational advantages and new worldwide opportunities. The adaptation of these basic institutions to take advantage of their societies' opportune situations ignited the greatest burst of sustained economic growth the world has yet seen.

Once these forces came together, individual drive for achievement was further strengthened by other factors found in non-Confucian societies as well. These forces—consumerism, export orientation, and the success cycle—round out our understanding of why individuals in these societies remain so dynamic.

Consumerism, the passionate drive to acquire new goods, was especially strong in East Asia. Goods produced there for export could be observed locally, and the rapid increase in East Asian income quickly brought these new goods within the reach of the local population. Before industrialization began in these five societies, one could observe in them a measure of resignation about the acquisition of new consumer goods. Most people knew about the existence of various modern products, but generally assumed that the goods were beyond their grasp—that the chance of acquiring them was so remote that there was little point in trying.

But consumers' passion for acquisition grew as products came within their reach. Each family focused on the next round of products to which it could reasonably aspire. In early rounds, families were excited by products such as sewing machines, watches, bicycles, radios, cameras, and tile roofs. They moved on to telephones, televisions, refrigerators, washing machines, and electric rice cookers, and then to heating or air conditioning, automobiles, and larger dwellings with more modern fixtures. The passion may have derived from many factors—desire for convenience, avoidance of back-breaking labor, curiosity, entertainment, the excitement of a new fad, the constant stimulation from new advertisements—but it was also driven by the desire to keep up socially with one's friends and neighbors and has been kept in bounds by what they considered proper.

Once an East Asian nation made a firm commitment to increase exports, the pressure to keep down costs to meet the global competition pushed them to achieve higher and higher levels of performance. Countries in Europe have an advantage in exporting to nearby countries because of low transportation costs, but East Asian countries had to compete in overseas markets where they had no special advantage of location, language, or traditional ties, and often suffered an initial disadvantage. Competition in, and dependence on, world markets required production standards higher than those needed to satisfy domestic markets, forcing East Asian countries to continue to scan the world for relevant information, to rush to absorb new technology, to improve productivity and quality, and to reduce costs. The pressures felt keenly by the East Asian company have, in turn, been passed on to the worker, whose job and welfare depend on his or her company's success.

The success of East Asians in meeting this competition in international markets has given East Asian countries, companies, and individuals a confidence in their own abilities, and this further fuels their determination to continue their efforts. In each round of success, they acquire new skills and new technology that often have broader applicability, and the added excitement helps propel them forward to another round. These factors—consumerism, export orientation, and the cycle of success—though not unique to East Asia, have helped reinforce the situational and cultural factors to sustain the drive for achievement.

The End of an Era

Although the dynamism continues, Japan and the four little dragons have begun to undergo basic changes,[15] changes sufficiently fundamental that in the early 1990s we may speak of the end of the era of industrial breakthrough. Signs of basic change began to appear in Japan in the 1970s, after the first oil shock, and in four little dragons in the late 1980s, after their currencies rose in value against the U.S. dollar. These changes help us see the nature of these societies during their several decades of industrial breakthrough in sharper relief. Some of the major new trends are as follows.

The End of Cheap Labor   East Asia's cheap labor supply has ended. The pool of poor immigrants dislocated by war has dried up, and the number of rural youth so desperate for employment that they are willing to accept long hours of physical exertion at low wages has dwindled. The portion of Japanese working in agriculture had dropped from 50 percent immediately after World War II to below 10 percent by the late 1980s; in Taiwan and South Korea, it had dropped from more than 60 percent to below 20 percent. Illegal immigrants are trickling into all of these societies, but thus far they constitute less than 1 percent of the work force and do not significantly ease the labor shortage. With labor shortages, wages have risen and the era when these economies enjoyed a major competitive advantage from low wages is over.

Accumulation of Sizable Financial Assets   By the late 1980s the economies of Japan and the four little dragons had accumulated sizable financial assets. The widespread availability of capital in these societies has led to great changes in the strategy of firms, in government-business relations, and in individual consumption patterns.

As firms have accumulated more capital, they are giving more attention to financial management. Some large manufacturing firms now have such sizable assets that they require fund managers simply to handle their company investments. Companies once run by engineers today have more executives trained in accounting. Companies that once decided to build new industrial facilities if they possessed the requisite technological and management skills now calculate costs more precisely.

When capital and foreign exchange were in short supply, the governments in these societies had great leverage over private firms in allocating and approving use of foreign currency, making available tax incentives and low-interest loans, and signaling priority areas so that private banks could lend at lower rates because of reduced financial risk. As firms have accumulated financial reserves of their own, including assets abroad, they have become less dependent on government assistance and less responsive to government directives.

As capital became more readily available for local investment, governments relaxed controls on the export of capital, and firms rapidly expanded their investment overseas. As firms headquartered in East Asia invest abroad and form more alliances with foreign companies to increase their global production and marketing, their interests are beginning to diverge from national interests. As of the early 1990s this process is still at an early stage in East Asia. Bureaucrats still have considerable leverage over firms based in their own country, but the leverage is far less complete than it once was.

The accumulation of capital is also affecting private consumption behavior. In the early years of industrialization, families increased their consumer purchases less rapidly than they accumulated wealth. They saved for retirement, for housing, for emergencies, for major purchases, and for their children's education. After the mid-1980s, as East Asian currencies appreciated against the U.S. dollar, East Asians, already aware of economic conditions elsewhere, became more likely to measure their wealth against what it could buy abroad. Those with assets in stocks and real estate, viewing their greatly expanded assets, became more willing to borrow against these assets to spend. This inclination fueled vast new spending and helped further ignite a bidding war for attractive investments. The price of stocks in local stock markets and the price of real estate, especially for land located in and around large cities, skyrocketed. Even the later bursting of some bubbles has not fully ended the bidding war.

Once prices of real estate leaped upward, the social cleavage between those who possessed property and those who did not became much sharper. In the early stages of industrialization, when there was little wealth in the society, a person's opportunities depended overwhelmingly on his or her job. But as wealth accumulated, many people could earn far more through investment and speculation than through their jobs. In Singapore, where ample publicly built real estate was available, property ownership did not loom as a large problem; but in Japan and the other little dragons, as real estate prices exploded, many young couples whose income depended on employment gave up the hope of ever acquiring their own homes. These new problems of inequality raised questions about social justice and, among some, created doubts about the basic social system.

The Growth of Finance and Other Services   Finance and other services have grown at the expense of industry. Just as the proportion of people engaged in agriculture dropped markedly in all modern societies as technological advances increased the efficiency of agriculture, so the advances of industry are now beginning to lessen the proportion of workers required for industry. Even though these five East Asian societies are expanding production and are supplying an increasing proportion of the world's industrial products, the advances in automation and in computer control of the production process are proceeding so rapidly that the number of workers required in industry is declining. To some extent, the jobs in labor-intensive industrial production have been passed on to other countries. But in Japan and the four little dragons, the proportion of the labor force actually engaged in industrial production has already peaked and is now beginning to decline.

The proportion of workers engaged in finance and other services, including government services, has continued to rise as young people look for their careers in these sectors. Just as the nature of society changed when stable farm societies gave way to industrial ones, so too as industry gives way to finance, the values of the industrial breakthrough era—regularity, precision, predictability, and coordination—are at least in part giving way to the values of finance—speculation, shrewd playing of the market, and willingness to take greater risks.

A More Vocal Public The public in these East Asian societies has begun demanding a greater voice in government. As people have acquired a better understanding of national and international affairs, gained exposure to Western television and foreign travel, and begun to see themselves as middle class, they have also begun to develop their own opinions and to raise questions about the nature of government policy.

The public has become particularly vocal about a host of new problems created directly or indirectly by industrialization: pollution, environmental damage, overcrowding, traffic congestion, loss of community, neglect of the aged, and increased chronic diseases in an increasingly aging population.

The events in the Philippines in 1986, when public demonstrations forced out Ferdinand Marcos, and the changes in the Soviet Union and Eastern Europe beginning in 1988 had a profound impact on East Asian countries. Because the authoritarian order in East Asia had been tightly linked to the cause of anti-communism, the more relaxed international political atmosphere undermined the East Asian justification for tight government controls. People have become less willing to tolerate secrecy and military control, and increasingly confident that their governments will eventually grant the public more freedoms.

The winds of democracy have grown stronger in all four of the little dragons. Before his death in 1988, Chiang Ching-kuo ended military rule and permitted a legal opposition in Taiwan, a policy that had a great impact. In June of 1987 when Roh Tae Woo announced that he was giving in to democratic demands, politics in South Korea were revolutionized. In Hong Kong, the events of Tiananmen in June 1989 set off massive public demonstrations as people sought more assurance regarding the methods that would safeguard popular local rule after 1997. Although changes were less dramatic in Singapore, even there, voters in the 1980s became more willing to vote for the opposition and expressed a desire for a new and younger leadership. In all these countries, the constraints against public expression of divergent views have been loosened and the demands for a genuine multiparty system have grown stronger.

The bureaucrats in these societies still have more power than their counterparts in modern Western societies, but the power of the public and of politicians who represent the public is increasing relative to that of the bureaucrats.

The winds of democracy have also been felt on the factory floor, as labor has begun to demand more rights. The changes have been most dramatic in South Korea, where days lost to strikes in 1987 were greater than they had been in the previous twenty-five years combined, but workers in Taiwan, Hong Kong, and Singapore have also begun to lose their docility.

CHANGES OF THIS SORT and magnitude indicate that the type of society that existed during the industrial breakthrough—with bureaucratic-authoritarian governments and meek publics, eager laborers who worked for low wages, companies that made their decisions with little regard to finance, and tight links between national and corporate interests—is already being rapidly transformed. These societies are still significantly different from Western ones, but they are becoming more complex and diversified, more open, and less tightly disciplined.

The Impact of East Asian Industrialization outside East Asia

The East Asian industrial breakthrough that is now drawing to a close has already had a profound impact on the world. The success of the East Asian economies has stimulated peoples around the world to raise their expectations concerning economic improvement and has changed the nature of analysis concerning how best to improve their nations' economies. The alteration in national consciousness in these countries is so complex that one cannot isolate specific causes in a way that would satisfy the scientific appetite for precise measurement. Yet those of us who follow East Asian success and the world's reaction to it are convinced that the changes are no less real.

The impact in the Communist world has been particularly profound. In China, once the doors to the world began to open in the 1970s, news of progress by Japan, Korea, and above all by Chinese populations in Taiwan, Hong Kong, and Singapore was a powerful stimulus for reform. In the Soviet Union and Eastern Europe, it had been possible to explain the more prosperous Western economies as resulting from historical differences that long antedated the Communist system. But when members of the Soviet bloc observed East Asian countries coming from behind and passing them in industrial development, it was difficult not to raise questions about their own system.

In the southern hemisphere, East Asian countries cannot match the appeal of the United States in its democracy, concern for human rights, receptiveness to foreigners, or creativity in popular culture. But the success of East Asian economies is beginning to create an interest in southern tier countries that goes beyond the pragmatic desire for funds and technology. East Asia is increasingly seen as an appealing model for catching up with the Western economies, for avoiding excessive decadence and crime, for overcoming the stalemates created by vested interests, and for enabling local customs to survive the onslaught of Western domination. Nations in the southern hemisphere are displaying increased interest in using the lessons of East Asian countries to improve their own educational systems and their own standards of living.

In North America and Europe, East Asian investment is beginning to have a powerful impact. By 1990 Indiana, for example, had over eighty separate Japanese factories, although Japanese investment in Indiana lags far behind that in California, New York, Georgia, Kentucky, Tennessee, Ohio, and several other states. Unlike most American firms overseas, which are turned over to local management, most Japanese factories abroad are tightly controlled by Japanese managers, bringing Japanese attitudes into the factories and down to the working level. Japanese purchases of foreign property and foreign companies, on the one hand, and large numbers of Japanese tourists, on the other, lead companies and tourist services around the world to adapt to Japanese tastes. Heads of governments and U.S. state governors seeking investments are becoming supplicants to Japan and other East Asian countries. Former American public officials, hired by the Japanese, have become Japan's agents for influencing American public policy.

In particular, the extraordinary competitiveness of companies from Japan is forcing Western companies around the world to learn from the Japanese new technology and management techniques such as quality control and inventory management. Signs of deeper institutional change are also beginning to appear. In the United States, antitrust rules are being relaxed so that companies in the same sector may cooperate on research projects, and new public-private cooperative projects are being considered. Large companies, keenly aware of their Japanese competitors, are experimenting with new kinds of relationships with suppliers to improve quality and speed up the time required for producing new products. Those who are working to shape the European Economic Community beyond 1992 acknowledge that competition from Japan helped create the union and will force it to adapt.

Just as in the late nineteenth century in Japan there was an attempt to preserve the Japanese spirit while absorbing Western technology, so Westerners remain slow in changing their fundamental conceptions. The idea that the free and open market is the best way to make decisions remains one of the few beliefs that in many Western countries approaches a secular article of faith, but even it is fraying at the edges. There are signs that the kinds of cooperation and strategy coming from East Asia are rapidly overtaking Westerners who believe that decisions should be made entirely by the "market" and the quarterly balance sheet.

In international affairs, too, East Asian countries are increasing their role and influence. In international organizations concerned with economic assistance and public health, for example, the Japanese are not only contributing more financially but are assuming higher offices and participating more in the policymaking.

Finally, a word about the impact of East Asia on the academic world. There is a great increase in the number of non-Asians studying East Asia, and this is beginning to have an effect on intellectual perspectives generally. Some pet theories, such as versions of dependency theory that maintain that the world's "core" areas, Western Europe and North America, are keeping the rest of the world from developing, may need even further reexamination.

But complex structural changes are occurring even in the

nature of modern East Asian studies. Just as many who have studied traditional culture in East Asia are frustrated that the world they knew and loved has been destroyed by industrial and commercial development, so the East Asianists who formerly dominated modern East Asian studies must acknowledge that the field is irreparably changed. The successful industrial transformation of East Asia has made the area of interest not only to East Asia specialists but to academics and to practitioners in the fields of world politics, finance, industrial organization, technology, and science. Some scholars are nostalgic for the days when their academic field was smaller, more manageable, and of less interest to scholars in other fields. A problem exists much like that of the State Department, where some area specialists mourn bygone days when diplomats had more room to maneuver and complain that they must now work with people in many different government branches, including Congress, who do not have the expertise to match their power. Scholars whose primary academic focus is contemporary East Asia must today wrestle with new realities that require them to interact with scholars and practitioners in other fields, many of whom are not well trained in East Asian culture. To work with them effectively and to help them perform their own jobs better, we must help raise their level of knowledge about the region. Even more than before, therefore, we have an obligation to emulate Edwin Reischauer and John Fairbank, the great pioneers in educating nonspecialists about East Asia.

Notes / Index

Notes

1. A New Wave of Industrialization

1. According to World Bank figures, Japan ranked third in merchandise trade, Hong Kong tenth, South Korea eleventh, Taiwan thirteenth, and Singapore seventeenth. *Far Eastern Economic Review*, August 16, 1990, 55.

2. For a recent review of various explanations for Western progress, see Daniel Chirot, "The Rise of the West," *American Sociological Review* 50 (1985): 181–195. Western scholars have been slow to recognize the extent of East Asian industrial development. For example, few Western scholars recall that Japan became a competitive industrial challenger before World War II. For an exception, a book written before World War II, see G. E. Hubbard, *Eastern Industrialization and Its Effect on the West, with Special Reference to Great Britain and Japan* (London: Oxford Univ. Press, 1935).

3. For an account of different perspectives, see Chapter 1 in Gregory W. Noble, "Between Competition and Collaboration: Collective Action in the Industrial Policy of Japan and Taiwan" (Ph.D. diss., Harvard Univ., 1988). See also Gregory W. Noble, "The Japanese Industrial Policy Debate," in *Pacific Dynamics: The International Politics of Industrial Change,* ed. Stephan Haggard and Chung-in Moon (Boulder: Westview Press, 1989); Robert Wade, *Governing the Market: Economic Theory and the Role of Government in East Asian Industrialization* (Prince-

ton: Princeton Univ. Press, 1990); and Stephan Haggard, *Pathways from the Periphery: The Politics of Growth in the Newly Industrializing Countries* (Ithaca: Cornell Univ. Press, 1990). For different theories as applied to Taiwan, see Edwin A. Winckler and Susan Greenhalgh, eds., *Contending Approaches to the Political Economy of Taiwan* (Armonk, N.Y.: M. E. Sharpe, 1988). For an argument linking Japanese modernization to Confucianism, see Michio Morishima, *Why Has Japan Succeeded?* (New York: Cambridge Univ. Press, 1982).

4. Karl Polanyi, *The Great Transformation: The Political and Economic Origins of Our Times* (1944; reprint, Boston: Beacon, 1957).

5. Alfred Stepan argues, for example, that Peru had a very effective economic strategy except that it failed to raise sufficient capital domestically. Alfred Stepan, *The State and Society: Peru in Comparative Perspective* (Princeton: Princeton Univ. Press, 1978).

6. See Daniel Chirot, *Social Change in the Modern Era* (New York: Harcourt Brace Jovanovich, 1986).

7. I. M. Destler, *American Trade Politics* (Washington, D.C.: Institute for International Economics, 1986), 40–41. See also Richard Rosecrance, *The Rise of the Trading State: Commerce and Conquest in the Modern World* (New York: Basic Books, 1986).

2. Taiwan

1. *Chung-hua min-kuo t'ung-chi t'i-kao* (Taipei: Directorate-General of Budgets, Accounts, and Statistics, 1955).

2. Ching-yuan Lin, *Industrialization in Taiwan, 1946–1972: Trade and Import-Substitution Policies for Developing Countries* (New York: Praeger, 1979), 47.

3. Quoted in Lin, *Industrialization in Taiwan,* p. 63.

4. For accounts of this period see Samuel P. S. Ho, *Economic Development of Taiwan, 1860–1970* (New Haven: Yale Univ. Press, 1978), 186–195; Gustav Ranis, "Industrial Development," in *Economic Growth and Structural Change in Taiwan: The Postwar Experience of the Republic of China,* ed. Walter

Galenson (Ithaca: Cornell Univ. Press, 1979), 209–218; Lin, *Industrialization in Taiwan;* Robert Wade, *Governing the Market: Economic Theory and the Role of Government in East Asian Industrialization* (Princeton: Princeton Univ. Press, 1990). For a historical account of local business, see Donald R. DeGlopper, "Doing Business in Lukang," in *Economic Organization in Chinese Society,* ed. William E. Willmott (Stanford: Stanford Univ. Press, 1972), 297–326.

5. For a summary of its economic mismanagement, see Suzanne Pepper, *Civil War in China: The Political Struggle, 1945–1949* (Berkeley: Univ. of California Press, 1978), 95–131.

6. See Fred Riggs, *Formosa under Chinese Nationalist Rule* (New York: Macmillan, 1952); and John Israel, "Politics on Formosa," in *Formosa Today,* ed. Mark Mancall (New York: Praeger, 1964), 59–67.

7. Edwin A. Winckler, "Elite Political Struggle, 1945–1985," in *Contending Approaches to the Political Economy of Taiwan,* ed. Edwin A. Winckler and Susan Greenhalgh (Armonk, N.Y.: M. E. Sharpe, 1988), 156–157. This article contains an excellent account of the early political efforts to consolidate rule. See also Hung-mao Tien, *The Great Transition: Political and Social Change in the Republic of China* (Stanford: Hoover Institution Press, 1989). For an interesting account of the political struggles underlying the fight between the financial cliques and the industrial builders, see Wade, *Governing the Market,* 387–393. For the first two decades after 1945, see George H. Kerr, *Formosa Betrayed* (Boston: Houghton Mifflin, 1965).

8. For an account of how Chiang Ching-kuo was broadening his power base, written before he succeeded his father, see J. Bruce Jacobs, "Recent Leadership and Political Trends in Taiwan," *China Quarterly,* no. 45 (1971): 129–154. See also Kerr, *Formosa Betrayed,* 393–396.

9. For an account of the incident and its background, see Kerr, *Formosa Betrayed.*

10. See J. Bruce Jacobs, *Local Politics in a Rural Chinese Cultural Setting: A Field Study of Mazu Township, Taiwan* (Canberra: Contemporary China Centre, Australian National Univ., 1980);

and John F. Copper and George P. Chen, *Taiwan's Elections: Political Development and Democratization in the Republic of China* (Baltimore: School of Law, Univ. of Maryland, 1984).

11. Edwin A. Winckler, "Institutionalization and Participation on Taiwan: From Hard to Soft Authoritarianism?" *China Quarterly*, no. 99 (1984): 481–499.

12. See Ho, *Economic Development of Taiwan*, 112–114; Lin, *Industrialization in Taiwan*, 33–38; and Erik Lundberg, "Fiscal and Monetary Policies," in *Economic Growth and Structural Change*, ed. Galenson, 263–307.

13. For accounts of land reform, see Sung-hsing Wang and Raymond Apthorpe, *Rice Farming in Taiwan: Three Village Studies* (Taipei: Institute of Ethnology, Academia Sinica, 1974); Hsin-Huang Michael Hsiao, *Government Agricultural Strategies in Taiwan and South Korea* (Taipei: Institute of Ethnology, Academia Sinica, 1981); Martin M. C. Yang, *Socio-Economic Results of Land Reform in Taiwan* (Honolulu: East-West Center, Univ. of Hawaii, 1967); Bernard Gallin, *Hsin Hsing, Taiwan: A Chinese Village in Change* (Berkeley: Univ. of California Press, 1966); Ho, *Economic Development of Taiwan*, 147–185; Erik Thorbecke, "Agricultural Development," in *Economic Growth and Structural Change*, ed. Galenson, 132–205; Burton Pasternak, *Kinship and Community in Two Chinese Villages* (Stanford: Stanford Univ. Press, 1973); and Ch'en Ch'eng, *Land Reform in Taiwan* (Taipei: China Publishing Co., 1961).

14. For accounts of agricultural progress under the Japanese, see Ramon Myers and Adrienne Ching, "Agricultural Development in Taiwan under Japanese Rule," *Journal of Asian Studies*, 23 (1964): 555–570; and Edgar Wickberg, "Continuities in Land Tenure, 1900–1940," in *The Anthropology of Taiwanese Society*, ed. Emily Martin Ahern and Hill Gates (Stanford: Stanford Univ. Press, 1981), 212–238.

15. Neil H. Jacoby, *U.S. Aid to Taiwan: A Study of Foreign Aid, Self-Help, and Development* (New York: Praeger, 1966); Ralph N. Clough, *Island China* (Cambridge: Harvard Univ. Press, 1978).

16. For Lee's early academic work, which shows the flow of funding from agriculture to industry, see Teng-hui Lee, *Intersectoral Flows in the Economic Development of Taiwan, 1895–1960* (Ithaca: Cornell Univ. Press, 1971). For an account of the JCRR, see Joseph A. Yager, *Transforming Agriculture in Taiwan: The Experience of the Joint Commission on Rural Reconstruction* (Ithaca: Cornell Univ. Press, 1988).

17. Clough, *Island China,* 79; Ho, *Economic Development of Taiwan,* 113.

18. Ramon H. Myers and Mark R. Peattie, *The Japanese Colonial Empire, 1895–1945* (Princeton: Princeton Univ. Press, 1984).

19. For an account of the highly developed marketing network early in Taiwan's Kuomintang period, see Lawrence W. Crissman, "Marketing on the Changhua Plain, Taiwan," in *Economic Organization in Chinese Society,* ed. Willmott, 215–259. For a general account of improvements during the Japanese colonial era, see Neil H. Jacoby, *An Evaluation of Aid to Free China* (Washington, D.C.: AID Bureau for the Far East, 1966).

20. E. Patricia Tsurumi, *Japanese Colonial Education in Taiwan, 1895–1945* (Cambridge: Harvard Univ. Press, 1977).

21. Even mountainous areas were fairly commercialized by the beginning of Japanese colonization. See, for example, Stevan Harrell, *Ploughshare Village: Culture and Context in Taiwan* (Seattle: Univ. of Washington Press, 1982).

22. See Ho, *Economic Development of Taiwan;* and Myers and Peattie, eds., *The Japanese Colonial Empire.*

23. Jacoby, *An Evaluation of Aid to Free China.*

24. Quoted in Lin, *Industrialization in Taiwan,* 26.

25. For an account of the economic decisions in the transition from import substitution to export promotion, see Lin, *Industrialization in Taiwan.* See also Chien-kuo Pang, "The State and Economic Transformation: The Taiwan Case" (Ph.D. diss., Brown Univ., 1988), 122ff.

26. Pang, "The State and Economic Transformation," 122ff.

27. K. T. Li, *The Experience of Dynamic Economic Growth on Taiwan* (Taipei: Meiya Publications, 1976).

28. See Jacoby, *U.S. Aid to Taiwan;* Clough, *Island China;* and

Richard Barrett, "Autonomy and Diversity in the American State on Taiwan," in *Contending Approaches,* ed. Winckler and Greenhalgh, 121–137.

29. For a brief account of the role of K. Y. Yin and K. T. Li, see Pang, "The State and Economic Transformation," 65–69, 184–185. See also K. T. Li, *The Evolution of Policy behind Taiwan's Development Success* (New Haven: Yale Univ. Press, 1981); and K. T. Li, *Economic Transformation of Taiwan* (London: Shepheard-Walwyn Ltd., 1988).

30. Alan P. L. Liu, *Phoenix and the Lame Lion* (Stanford: Hoover Institution, 1987), 48ff.

31. William C. Kirby, "Continuity and Change in Modern China: Economic Planning on the Mainland and on Taiwan," *Australian Journal of Chinese Affairs,* no. 24 (July 1990): 1–20. See also William C. Kirby, *The International Development of China since 1928: Nationalist Industrial Policy and Its Heirs* (Stanford: Stanford Univ. Press, 1991).

32. For accounts of economic policy and development, see Ho, *Economic Development of Taiwan;* Galenson, ed., *Economic Growth and Structural Change;* Shirley W. Y. Kuo, *The Taiwan Economy in Transition* (Boulder: Westview Press, 1983); and Lin, *Industrialization in Taiwan.*

33. Liu, *Phoenix and the Lame Lion,* 51.

34. For biographical information on these leaders, see Pang, "The State and Economic Transformation."

35. For K. T. Li's accounts of policies, see his *The Experience of Dynamic Economic Growth on Taiwan; The Evolution of Policy behind Taiwan's Development Success;* and *Economic Transformation of Taiwan.*

36. Pang, "The State and Economic Transformation," 76.

37. Liu, *Phoenix and the Lame Lion,* 122ff.

38. Janne E. Nolan, *Military Industry in Taiwan and South Korea* (New York: St. Martin's Press, 1986).

39. Gregory W. Noble, "Between Competition and Collaboration: Collective Action in the Industrial Policy of Japan and Taiwan" (Ph.D. diss., Harvard Univ., 1988).

40. See Gregory W. Noble, "Contending Forces in Taiwan's Economic Policymaking," *Asian Survey* (June 1987): 683–704; and Nolan, *Military Industry in Taiwan and South Korea.*

41. Thomas B. Gold, "Entrepreneurs, Multinationals, and the State," in *Contending Approaches,* ed. Winckler and Greenhalgh, 190.

42. Thomas B. Gold, *State and Society in the Taiwan Miracle* (Armonk, N.Y.: M. E. Sharpe, 1986), 71.

43. Gold, "Entrepreneurs, Multinationals, and the State," 188.

44. Liu, *Phoenix and the Lame Lion,* 125–145.

45. Gold, *State and Society in the Taiwan Miracle.*

46. Gallin, *Hsin Hsing.*

47. See, for example, Gallin, *Hsin Hsing.*

48. Robert H. Silin, *Leadership and Values: The Organization of Large-Scale Taiwanese Enterprises* (Cambridge: East Asian Research Center, Harvard Univ., 1976). See also Stephen M. Olsen, "The Inculcation of Economic Values in Taipei Business Families," in *Economic Organization in Chinese Society,* ed. Willmott, 261–295. For the changes in attitude among young factory workers, see Lydia Kung, "Perceptions of Work among Factory Women," in *The Anthropology of Taiwanese Society,* ed. Ahern and Gates; and Lydia Kung, *Factory Women in Taiwan* (Ann Arbor: UMI Research Press, 1983). For other accounts of changes in Taiwanese society, see other articles in the Ahern and Gates volume, and James C. Hsiung, ed., *The Taiwan Experience* (New York: American Association for Chinese Studies, 1981).

49. Myron L. Cohen, *House United, House Divided: The Chinese Family in Taiwan* (New York: Columbia Univ. Press, 1967); Margery Wolf, *The House of Lim: A Study of a Chinese Farm Family* (New York: Appleton-Century-Crofts, 1968); and Lung-shen Shung, "Property and Family Division," in *The Anthropology of Chinese Society,* ed. Ahern and Gates, 361–378.

50. Gold, *State and Society in the Taiwan Miracle,* 128ff. See also Chi Schive, *The Foreign Factor: The Multinational Corporation's Contribution to the Economic Modernization of the Republic of China* (Stanford: Hoover Institution Press, 1990).

51. Sheng-huo Su-chi Yen-chiu Chung-hsin, ed., *Chung-hua Min-kuo Ti-i Tz'u She-hui Pao-kao* (Taipei, 1985), 81.
52. Ibid., 19.
53. For an account of some of these international changes and the impact on Taiwan, see Harvey Feldman and Ilpyong J. Kim, eds., *Taiwan in a Time of Transition* (New York: Paragon, 1988).
54. See Ranis, "Industrial Development."

3. South Korea

1. For an overview of Korean history, including an excellent account of post-war history, see Carter J. Eckert, Ki-baik Lee, Young Ick Lew, Michael Robinson, and Edward W. Wagner, *Korea Old and New: A History* (Cambridge: Korea Institute, Harvard Univ., 1990).
2. For annual estimates of per capita income for South Korea, Taiwan, Japan, and the United States, see Byung-Nak Song, *The Rise of the Korean Economy* (New York: Oxford Univ. Press, 1990), 80.
3. For a sympathetic and intimate account of Rhee, see Robert T. Oliver, *Syngman Rhee and American Involvement in Korea, 1942–1960* (Seoul: Panmun Book Co., 1978). See also Harold Joyce Noble, in *Embassy at War,* ed. Frank Baldwin (Seattle: Univ. of Washington Press, 1975). For a more critical view, see Frank Baldwin, ed., *Without Parallel: The American-Korean Relationship since 1945* (New York: Pantheon, 1974).
4. See, for example, Man-gap Lee, *Sociology and Social Change in Korea* (Seoul: Seoul National Univ. Press, 1982), 32.
5. See, for example, Bruce Cumings, *The Origins of the Korean War,* vol. 2: *The Roaring of the Cataract, 1947–1950* (Princeton: Princeton Univ. Press, 1990).
6. Bruce Cumings, *The Origins of the Korean War,* vol. 1: *Liberation and the Emergence of Separate Regimes, 1945–1947* (Princeton: Princeton Univ. Press, 1981); Cumings, *The Origins of the Korean War,* vol. 2. For the origins of the Communist

movement and an analysis of North Korea, see Robert Scalapino and Chong-sik Lee, *Communism in Korea,* 2 vols. (Berkeley: Univ. of California Press, 1972).

7. Quee-Young Kim, *The Fall of Syngman Rhee,* Korea Research Monograph no. 7 (Berkeley: Institute of East Asian Studies, Univ. of California, 1983).

8. For accounts of the political system, see Sungjoo Han, *The Failure of Democracy in South Korea* (Berkeley: Univ. of California Press, 1974); Joungwan A. Kim, *Divided Korea: The Politics of Development, 1945–1972* (Cambridge: Harvard Univ. Press, 1975); Ilpyong J. Kim and Young Whan Kihl, *Political Change in South Korea* (New York: Paragon, 1988); Young Whan Kihl, *Politics and Policies in Divided Korea: Regimes in Contest* (Boulder: Westview, 1984); Dae-Sook Suh and Chae-Jin Lee, eds., *Political Leadership in Korea* (Seattle: Univ. of Washington Press, 1976); and Bun Woong Kim and Wha Joon Rho, eds., *Korean Public Bureaucracy* (Seoul: Kyobo Publishing, 1982). For an account of attitudes of educated Koreans concerning political and economic modernization, see Sung Chick Hong, *The Intellectual and Modernization: A Study of Korean Attitudes* (Seoul: Social Research Institute, Korea Univ., 1967).

9. For an account of international developments as they affected Korea's internal politics and policies, see Ralph N. Clough, *Embattled Korea: The Rivalry for International Support* (Boulder: Westview, 1987).

10. For an analysis of the role of military in administration, see Hahn-been Lee, *Korea: Time, Change, and Administration* (Honolulu: East-West Center, 1968), 144–175.

11. Lee, *Korea: Time, Change, and Administration.* See also Vincent S. R. Brandt, "Korea," in *Ideology and National Competitiveness: An Analysis of Nine Countries,* ed. George C. Lodge and Ezra F. Vogel (Cambridge: Harvard Business School Press, 1987), 218.

12. For example, see David C. Cole and Princeton N. Lyman, *Korean Development: The Interplay of Politics and Economics* (Cambridge: Harvard Univ. Press, 1971), 36.

13. Chung H. Lee and Tuvia Blumenthal, "Introduction," in *The Economic Development of Japan and Korea,* ed. Chung H. Lee and Ippei Yamazawa (New York: Praeger, 1990).

14. See Noel F. McGinn, Donald R. Snodgrass, and Young Bong Kim, *Education and Development in Korea,* Studies in the Modernization of the Republic of Korea, 1945–1975 (Cambridge: Council on East Asian Studies, Harvard Univ., 1980), esp. 150–151.

15. For an account of the Korean approach to both formal education and in-firm training, see Alice Amsden, *Asia's Next Giant* (New York: Oxford Univ. Press, 1989), 215–239.

16. In 1938, for example, in manufacturing, transport and storage, banking, and insurance, Japanese-run companies in Korea had more than eight times as much paid-in capital as Korean-run companies. Kwang Suk Kim and Michael Roemer, *Growth and Structural Transformation* (Cambridge: Council on East Asian Studies, Harvard Univ., 1979), 15.

17. Estimate by Prof. Katsuhiko Sakuma, of Tokyo University of Foreign Languages, who prepared Japanese-language teaching materials for Korea.

18. Clough, *Embattled Korea,* 40.

19. For a general account of the early years of Korean industrialization up to 1975, see Edward S. Mason, Mahn Je Kim, Dwight H. Perkins, Kwang Suk Kim, and David C. Cole, *The Economic and Social Modernization of the Republic of Korea* (Cambridge: Council on East Asian Studies, Harvard Univ., 1980). See also Chuk Kyo Kim, ed., *Individual and Social Development Issues* (Seoul: Korea Development Institute, 1977); and Hyun-Chin Lim, *Dependent Development in Korea, 1963–1979* (Seoul: Seoul National Univ. Press, 1985). More detailed information on various aspects of the economy is contained in the nine-volume series Studies in the Modernization of the Republic of Korea, 1945–1975 (Cambridge: Council on East Asian Studies, Harvard Univ.). For a more recent account of the Korean economy, see Byung-Nak Song, *The Rise of the Korean Economy* (New York: Oxford Univ. Press, 1990).

20. See Sun Hwan Ban, Pal Yong Moon, and Dwight H. Perkins,

Rural Development, Studies in the Modernization of the Republic of Korea, 1945–1975 (Cambridge: Council on East Asian Studies, Harvard Univ., 1980), esp. Vincent Brandt, "Local Government and Rural Development," 260–280, 283–297; and Hsin-Huang Michael Hsiao, *Government Agricultural Strategies in Taiwan and South Korea* (Taipei: Institute of Ethnology, Academia Sinica, 1981).

21. See, for example, Vincent S. R. Brandt, *A Korean Village between Farm and Sea* (Cambridge: Harvard Univ. Press, 1971).

22. Sun Hwan Ban, "Agricultural Growth in Korea, 1918–1971," in *Agricultural Growth in Japan, Taiwan, Korea, and the Philippines,* ed. Yujiro Hayami, Vernon W. Ruttan, and Herman M. Southworth (Honolulu: East-West Center, Univ. of Hawaii, 1981), 90–116.

23. Robert Wade, *Irrigation and Agricultural Politics in South Korea* (Boulder: Westview, 1982), 4, For an account of some of the changes in the countryside as a result of industrialization, see Clark W. Sorensen, *Over the Mountains Are Mountains: Korean Peasant Households and Their Adaptations to Rapid Industrialization* (Seattle: Univ. of Washington Press, 1988).

24. Lee, *Korea: Time, Change, and Administration,* 179.

25. For an account of Park's efforts to build up the defense industry, see Janne E. Nolan, *Military Industry in Taiwan and South Korea* (New York: St. Martin's Press, 1986).

26. See Han, *The Failure of Democracy in South Korea,* for a general account of political development.

27. Lee, *Korea: Time, Change, and Administration,* 157.

28. Samuel Ho, "South Korea and Taiwan," *Asian Survey,* 21 (December 1981), 196; Yung Whee Rhee, Bruce Ross-Larson, and Garry Pursell, *Korea's Competitive Edge: Managing the Entry into World Markets* (Baltimore: Johns Hopkins Univ. Press, 1984).

29. For an account of Taegu, see Man-gap Lee and Herbert R. Barringer, eds., *A City in Transition: Urbanization in Taegu, Korea* (Seoul: Hollym Corp., 1971).

30. See, for example, Kee Young Kim, "American Technology and Korea's Technological Development," 75–96, and Hak Chong Lee, "The American Role in the Development of Management Education in Korea," 177–195, both in *From Patron to Partner: The Development of U.S.-Korean Business and Trade Relations,* ed. Karl Moskowitz (Lexington, Mass.: Lexington Books, 1984).

31. Kwan Bong Kim, *The Korea-Japan Treaty Crisis and the Instability of the Korean Political System* (New York: Praeger, 1971).

32. For a general account of these topics, see Leroy P. Jones and Il Sakong, *Government, Business, and Entrepreneurship in Economic Development: The Korean Case,* Studies in the Modernization of the Republic of Korea, 1945–1975 (Cambridge: Council on East Asian Studies, Harvard Univ., 1980).

33. For accounts of the labor situation, see George Ewing Ogle, "Labor Unions in Rapid Economic Development: Case of the Republic of Korea in the 1960s" (Ph.D. diss., Univ. of Wisconsin, 1973); Park Young-ke, *Labor and Industrial Relations in Korea: System and Practice* (Seoul: Sogang Univ. Press, 1979); Jang Jip Choi, *Labor and the Authoritarian State: Labor Unions in South Korean Manufacturing Industries, 1961–1980* (Seoul: Korea Univ. Press, 1989); and Ezra F. Vogel and David L. Lindauer, "Toward a Social Compact for South Korean Labor," Discussion Paper no. 317, Harvard Institute for International Development, November 1989.

34. Edwin S. Mills and Byung-Nak Song, *Urbanization and Urban Problems,* Studies in the Modernization of the Republic of Korea, 1945–1975 (Cambridge: Council on East Asian Studies, Harvard Univ., 1979).

35. See Man-gap Lee, ed., *Toward a New Community Life: Reports of an International Relations Seminar on the "Saemaul Movement"* (Seoul: Institute of Saemaul Undong Studies, Seoul National Univ., 1981).

36. Mason et al., *Economic and Social Modernization,* 189.

37. For an overview comparing Japanese and South Korean foreign trade, see Lee and Yamazawa, eds., *The Economic Development of Japan and Korea,* 3–29.

38. See, for example, Tamio Hattori, *Kankoku no Keiei Hatten* (Tokyo: Bunshindoo, 1988).

39. For a comparison of Korea and Japan by economists, see Kim and Roemer, *Growth and Structural Transformation*, 137–146; and Lee and Yamazawa, eds., *The Economic Development of Japan and Korea.*

40. For an overview of Korean licensing of foreign technology from 1962 to 1976, see Lee and Blumenthal, "Introduction," in *The Economic Development of Japan and Korea,* ed. Lee and Yamazawa, xxiii.

41. For background on the Pohang Iron and Steel Company, see Amsden, *Asia's Next Giant,* 291–318.

42. See, for example, Tun-jen Cheng and Stephan Haggard, *Newly Industrializing Asia in Transition: Policy Reform and American Response,* Policy Paper no. 31 (Berkeley: Institute of International Studies, Univ. of California, 1987). Jung-en Woo makes a strong case that because a high proportion of foreign funds was channeled through the government, this helped strengthen state power and enabled the government to make available to selected private firms low-cost finance to hasten industrialization. Jung-en Woo, *Race to the Swift: State and Finance in Korean Industrialization* (New York: Columbia Univ. Press, 1991).

43. See Hattori, *Kankoku no Keiei Hatten;* Jones and Sakong, *Government, Business, and Entrepreneurship;* and Richard M. Steers, Yoo Keun Shin, and Gerardo R. Ungson, *The Chaebol: Korea's New Industrial Might* (New York: Harper and Row, 1989).

44. For a pioneering study of the pre-war origins of Korean capitalism, see Carter Eckert, *Offspring of Empire: The Kochiang Kims and the Colonial Origins of Korean Capitalism, 1876–1945* (Seattle: Univ. of Washington Press, 1991). See also Dennis L. McNamara, *The Colonial Origins of Korean Enterprise, 1910–1945* (New York: Cambridge Univ. Press, 1990).

45. Steers, Shin, and Ungson, *The Chaebol,* 91–92.

46. For accounts of Korean managers, see Kae H. Chung and Hak

Chong Lee, eds., *Korean Managerial Dynamics* (New York: Praeger, 1989); T. W. Kang, *Is Korea the Next Japan?* (New York: Free Press, 1989).

4. Hong Kong and Singapore

1. Siu-lun Wong, *Emigrant Entrepreneurs: Shanghai Industrialists in Hong Kong* (New York: Oxford Univ. Press, 1988). For a general bibliography on Hong Kong, see Ezra F. Vogel, *One Step Ahead in China: Guangdong under Reform* (Cambridge: Harvard Univ. Press, 1989), 483–484.
2. For a comprehensive encyclopedic overview of Singapore, which includes references to other works on Singapore, see Kernial Singh Sandhu and Paul Wheatley, eds., *Management of Success: The Moulding of Modern Singapore* (Singapore: Institute of Southeast Asian Studies, 1989).
3. Chan Heng-chee, "Politics in an Administrative State: Where Has the Politics Gone," in *Trends in Singapore,* ed. C. M. Seah (Singapore: Institute of Southeast Asian Studies, 1975).

5. Toward an Explanation

1. See, for example, Roy Hofheinz, Jr., and Kent E. Calder, *The Eastasia Edge* (New York: Basic Books, 1982); Chung-Hua Institution for Economic Research, *Conference on Confucianism and Economic Development in East Asia,* May 29–31, 1989 (Taipei, 1990); Hung-chao Tai, *Confucianism and Economic Development: An Oriental Alternative?* (Washington, D.C.: Washington Institute Press, 1989); Ronald P. Dore, "Confucianism, Economic Growth, and Social Development," in *In Search of an East Asian Development Model,* ed. Peter L. Berger and Hsin-Huang Michael Hsiao (New Brunswick, N.J.: Transaction Books, 1988); and Ronald Dore, *Taking Japan Seriously: A Confucian Perspective on Leading Economic Issues* (Stanford: Stanford Univ. Press, 1987). Michio Morishima, *Why Has Japan 'Succeeded'?: Western Technology and the Japanese Ethos* (New York: Cambridge Univ. Press, 1982).

2. For an account of Latin American industrialization contrasted with that of East Asia, see Gary Gereffi and Donald Wyman, "Determinants of Development Strategies in Latin America and East Asia," in *Pacific Dynamics: The International Politics of Industrial Change,* ed. Stephan Haggard and Chung-in Moon (Boulder: Westview, 1989). See also Stephan Haggard, *Pathways from the Periphery: The Politics of Growth in the Newly Industrializing Countries* (Ithaca: Cornell Univ. Press, 1990); and Ching-yuan Lin, *Latin America vs. East Asia: A Comparative Development Perspective* (Armonk, N.Y.: M. E. Sharpe, 1989).

3. For example, Mary Wright, in *The Last Stand of Chinese Conservatism* (Stanford: Stanford Univ. Press, 1957), 13, concludes that the late nineteenth-century effort at restoration failed because "the requirements of a modern state proved to run counter to the requirements of the Confucian order." Joseph Levenson found that specialization and professionalization needed for modernization were incompatible with the Confucian bureaucrat's amateur ideal. Joseph Levenson, *Confucian China and Its Modern Fate,* 2 vols. (Berkeley: Univ. of California Press, 1958, 1964).

4. Korea received approximately $6 billion in U.S. aid over three decades, beginning in 1945, and approximately $7 billion in U.S. military assistance. Edward S. Mason and Mahn Je Kim, "Preface," in *The Economic and Social Modernization of the Republic of Korea,* Edward S. Mason et al. (Cambridge: Council on East Asian Studies, Harvard Univ., 1980). Taiwan received from 1951 through 1967 about $1.5 billion in economic aid and about $2.5 billion in military assistance. Ian M. D. Little, "An Economic Reconnaissance," in *Economic Growth and Structural Change in Taiwan,* ed. Walter Galenson (Ithaca: Cornell Univ. Press, 1979), 457–458.

5. See Haggard, *Pathways from the Periphery;* Tun-jen Cheng and Stephan Haggard, *Newly Industrializing Asia in Transition* (Berkeley: Institute of International Studies, Univ. of California, 1987); Frederic C. Deyo, ed., *The Political Economy of the New Asian Industrialism* (Ithaca: Cornell Univ. Press, 1987);

Frederic C. Deyo, ed., *Beneath the Miracle: Labor Subordination in the New Asian Industrialism* (Berkeley: Univ. of California Press, 1989); Gordon White and Robert Wade, eds., *Developmental States in East Asia* (New York: St. Martin's Press, 1988); and Frederic C. Deyo, *Dependent Development and Industrial Order: An Asian Case Study* (New York: Praeger, 1981).

6. Lucian Pye has made a similar observation, noting that Confucianism previously emphasized ritual and status more than purposeful activity. Lucian W. Pye, *Asian Power and Politics: The Cultural Dimensions of Authority* (Cambridge: Harvard Univ. Press, 1985). See also Lucian Pye, *The Spirit of Chinese Politics: A Psychocultural Study of the Authority Crisis in Political Development* (Cambridge: MIT Press, 1968).

7. On issues related to transferability of Japanese patterns, see Robert A. Scalapino, Seizaburo Sato, and Jusuf Wanandi, eds., *Asian Economic Development—Present and Future* (Berkeley: Institute of East Asian Studies, Univ. of California, 1985); K. John Fukuda, *Japanese-Style Management Transferred: The Experience of East Asia* (London: Routledge, 1988); and T. W. Kang, *Is Korea the Next Japan?* (New York: Free Press, 1989).

8. On Confucianism, see Arthur F. Wright, *The Confucian Persuasion* (Stanford: Stanford Univ. Press, 1966); Benjamin Schwartz, *The World of Thought in Ancient China* (Cambridge: Harvard Univ. Press, 1985); and Tu Wei-ming, *Confucian Ethics Today: The Singapore Challenge* (Singapore: Federal Publications, 1984). On the psychological dimensions of Confucianism, see Richard H. Solomon, *Mao's Revolution and Chinese Political Culture* (Berkeley: Univ. of California Press, 1971); Richard Wilson, *Learning to Be Chinese: The Political Socialization of Chinese Children* (Cambridge: MIT Press, 1970); Pye, *Asian Power and Politics;* Michael Harris Bond, ed., *The Psychology of the Chinese People* (New York: Oxford Univ. Press, 1986); Donald Munro, ed., *Individualism and Holism: Studies in Confucian and Taoist Values* (Ann Arbor: Center for Chinese Studies, Univ. of Michigan, 1985); Irene Eber, ed., *Confu-*

cianism: The Dynamics of Tradition (New York: Macmillan, 1986); and Wei Ming Tu, "A Confucian Perspective on the Rise of Industrial East Asia," *Bulletin of the American Academy of Arts and Sciences* (October 1988): 32–50.

9. For a series of essays focusing on the adaptation of Confucian thought and institutions in the course of modernization, see Joseph P. L. Jiang, ed., *Confucianism and Modernization: A Symposium* (Taipei: Wu Nan Publishing Co., 1987). One excellent survey of early twentieth-century Chinese failures to industrialize points to problems of financial inadequacy and mismanagement rather than to the Confucian tradition; see Marie-Claire Bergere, *The Golden Age of the Chinese Bourgeoisie, 1911–1937* (New York: Cambridge Univ. Press, 1989).

10. Indeed, recent empirical studies of Chinese in Hong Kong and Taiwan find a greater authoritarianism than in comparable American and British subjects. See Yang Kuo-shu, "Chinese Personality and Its Change," in *The Psychology of the Chinese People,* ed. Bond, 126–129.

11. Recent empirical studies of Chinese in Hong Kong and Taiwan find more individualistic value orientations than these societies are believed to have had historically. See Yang Kuo-shu, "Chinese Personality and Its Change," and Michael Harris Bond and Kwang-Kuo Hwang, "The Social Psychology of Chinese People," in *The Psychology of the Chinese People,* ed. Bond.

12. For an account of relational networks in Chinese society, see Morton H. Fried, *The Fabric of Chinese Society: A Study of the Social Life of a Chinese County Seat* (reprint, New York: Octagon Books, 1969); Sidney L. Greenblatt, Richard W. Wilson, and Amy A. Wilson, eds., *Social Interaction in Chinese Society* (New York: Praeger, 1970).

13. Dore, *Taking Japan Seriously,* 17.

14. For accounts of the complex mix of values underlying group commitments in Taiwan and South Korea, see Edwin A. Winckler, "Statism and Familism on Taiwan," and Vincent S. R. Brandt, "Korea," in *Ideology and National Competitiveness: An Analysis of Nine Countries,* ed. George C. Lodge and

Ezra F. Vogel (Cambridge: Harvard Business School Press, 1986), 173–206 and 207–239.

15. For an account of some of the social changes resulting from modernization, see Sung Chick Hong, ed., *Consequences of Modernization and Social Development in Asian Societies* (Seoul: Asiatic Research Center, Korea Univ., 1987).

Index

2541